WILLIAM GIBSON

A SEASON IN HEAVEN

*being the log of
an expedition after that legendary beast,
cosmic consciousness*

New York ATHENEUM *1974*

for our two sons,
the believer and the doubter

A SEASON IN HEAVEN

I

A sentence I heard spoken forty years ago by a teacher of mine, now dead, lately has been echoing in my ear: "Sanity is to insanity as the shell is to the egg."

2

The experience begins with the four of us—my wife, me, our two adolescent sons—standing in line under a full moon along the docks of a river town in a corner of Spain. The river is black and full, spreading here into the Gulf of Cadiz; far across it glitter the lights of Portugal.

We are the only family in a crowd of some six hundred youth, from many countries, who have been gathering here out of chartered buses for a couple of hours. It is December, the night is chilly, and many of the young folk are hooded in blankets; the girls look like girls anywhere in their up-to-the-minute old-fashioned long skirts, but the boys are out of a catalogue, impeccable in dress shirts, neckties, and jackets, and not a beard or hank of long hair among them. A great many have flowers in hand—the rule is don't smell them, the unspoiled odor is essential—which they are careful with, as offerings-to-be. Quiety chatting, in queues under the streetlights between the warehouses and the river, all their faces are fresh, attractive, happy, and their manner is gentle and courteous, just what their parents hoped for. What they are awaiting is the

arrival of the master, and pending it their defer-
ence to our family takes me by surprise.

"Oh, you're a family," says a young man in
charge, "here, get on Maharishi's boat."

There are three ferry boats, and Maharishi's is the
prize; I say, "How come we rate such special treat-
ment?"

"Oh, Maharishi loves families," says the young
man, from the other side of the generation gap,
"what's more holy than the family?"

So we find ourselves in the passenger cabin, where
a table has been made ceremonial with a sheet, candles, and brass saucers, overseen by a portrait of a
cross-legged guru, and on a bench sit some bowls
of whipped cream and two dozen trays of home-
made gingerbread, like a church supper in Trenton.

All at once a profound silence breathes in from
the deck, where the crowd is on its feet, with palms
together, absolutely still; seeing my firstborn's hands
so, I blink and know for sure I am in the bowels of
some epiphany, and among the scores of heads I
glimpse Maharishi descending to the boat, by inches.
First in a group of figures in white dhotis, he is accepting flowers from the gauntlet of his disciples,
flower by flower, with a nod and a smile. He is
about five feet tall, with straggly black hair and a
full beard, its chin triangle white; his broad face
might be called sensual if it were less serene. The
crowd parting before him, he comes slowly onto
the ferry, and sits cross-legged at a place under the
pilothouse. The other figures in dhotis settle around

him; and then, not before, the crowd sits itself on the deck.

We put out into the river. The silence continues, until after half an hour the other two boats draw up on either side and are lashed to ours; now we have a single three-ferry raft with a multitude of six hundred gathered in a great semi-circle around Maharishi. The other engines are stilled, only ours with a quiet throbbing holds all three boats undrifting against the current in mid-river, and under the climbing moon the program begins.

As entertainment, which it isn't, it is pretty sparse. Maharishi, who has a degree in physics, is later quoted as having "said some complicated things about the moon"—folk poetry—such as that it sprang from the mind of the Creator, the moon is his left eye and the sun is his right. A public-address system is hooked up, and from time to time the other figures in dhotis break into Sanskrit chanting, beautiful and somewhat barbaric in the moonlight; a folk-rock duo sing some of their tender songs in praise of Maharishi and meditation, which my younger boy thinks are a bit "like commercials"; a poet begins to recite his verse, and when I hear how he wandered over Africa and Asia and it was all a big fantasia I retire into the cabin to check on the gingerbread. In due time, portions are passed out by a kitchen committee to everybody on the three decks. Nothing else except the intermittent silence takes place until around midnight, when the six hundred rise to their feet—many slip out of their shoes—to whisper in unison a Sanskrit "puja" for three minutes, after which all bow their heads to the deck. The night wind is getting uncomfortably cold, but as far as I can make out Maharishi has sat cross-legged in it for three hours without moving; that impresses me.

The boats are then unlashed, and separate to make their way back. Ours is last, and when we straggle onto the dock we wait there for Maharishi to follow because my older boy has a flower to offer—he's been trying in vain for a month, the queues too much for him—but Maharishi is now in the passenger cabin with the doors closed. After some thirty minutes word comes that he is making new initiators and will be another hour or two, the people should go home.

Which, back on the bus, we do.

This expedition has begun about six in the evening and run to almost two in the morning, half of those hours spent standing in line for buses, boats, and himself, a full night's work, and by no known standards was there a hot time in the old town tonight. Yet in the street next morning a woman I have a nodding acquantaince with stops to chat:

"Wasn't it beautiful? that boat ride alone was worth the whole fare from California."

I am baffled only for a moment, she also has a son in the movement. And a year or two earlier these hundreds of clean-cut youth were a good many of them unkempt in rags and spiritual disarray and drugs, believing in nothing—least of all in themselves. Of what elixir have they drunk now, what is this blossoming?

I don't hope to answer the question, merely—by noting odds and ends from the weeks I spent among them—to get rid of it.

3

A man calls up his local naturalist and says, "My cellar door was left open and I have a skunk living in the cellar, how do I get rid of it?" The naturalist says, "Skunks love breadcrumbs, take a fistful and make a trail of breadcrumbs from the cellar out through the open door into the field." Next day the man calls him up and says, "I did what you said," and the naturalist says, "Did it work?" and the man says, "Not quite, I now have two skunks."

In the final waiting on the dock a couple of the boatmen who were spitting in disgust over our voyage to nowhere—"Es ridiculo! es ridiculo!"—wanted their ferry back so they could go to bed. Turning to us, one asked:

"What passes there—adoration?"

My politic wife said, "Yes."

"Of God?" the boatman said.

She said, "Who else?"

"Ah," he said, with his face softening, and then explained, "In Spain we are all Christians."

I said, "Only since 1492."

Because in that year not only did Columbus sail out of this very coast for America, but the Moors were driven at last out of Granada; and Spain, united after centuries of religious and political divisions, entered upon its first century of greatness in world history—another blossoming out of disorder not irrelevant to my theme.

Skunk number two.

4

So I come to the breadcrumbs. I was there with my family because—

But let me introduce us parenthetically while I can; half of us will soon disappear from this travelogue, which is one of ideas, not family. Three of us have flown here from Massachusetts on a holiday. I am a writer—of plays, poems, other books—in my fifties, and my wife is a psychoanalyst, working now on a tome about the creative process; we have in tow our younger boy in jeans, a cool lad of sixteen, bearded and longhaired, soon to enter college as a math-and-science major. His moodier brother, once also in jeans and longhaired, and musically gifted, is now a shorn nineteen in suit and necktie who has declined college, and since fall taken up residence as a student here instead. It's his first long absence from home, it will last seven months, and the rest of us have dropped in to say hello at Christmas, casual-like.

The line of breadcrumbs is that we are all meditators; we practice "Transcendental Meditation"—introduced to the world by Maharishi Mahesh Yogi, and introduced to my wife and me by our children —and this is what the older boy is in Spain studying to become a teacher of. It was the younger who led us to our preparatory lecture and the older who, in the gloom of a thorny adolescence, was first initiated; after six months of meditating the relaxation in his face was unmistakable, and his brother joined up. My wife and I were not long after. One pays a fee—it ranges from $35 for highschool students to $75 for adults, part of which keeps the initiator alive, part the organization—and for fifteen days beforehand the nervous system must be clean of nonprescribed drugs. Since my lifetime experience with them consisted of one grass party, I was prompt to take my money and other offerings to my initiator. Fruit, flowers, a new handkerchief, she used them in a ceremony of thanks to the deceased masters, the "puja" I was later to hear on the ferry, and taught me a mantra and how to meditate with it.

The mantra is a Vedic sound without meaning, they say, selected for its suitability to the individual, and thereafter to be kept secret, like Rumpelstiltskin's name. If told, it loses its potency: this makes a kind of sense to me as a writer, I dislike talking about work in progress for fear of the same loss. Still, I wasn't sure the movement owned more than one mantra until I heard Maharishi say, "If your mantra has one syllable, or two, or three—" from which I deduced we had at least three, and maybe three billion, one for everyone.

Its use is so simple I am embarrassed to describe it, and luckily am pledged not to. I can say it is based on the natural drift of the mind; effort is the one way to go wrong. Doing as instructed in my initiation I experienced something unique, a letting go inside which was the first waking rest I'd had from myself in fifty years, and I went home to tell my wife, "You'll be surprised how potent it is." I was to meditate thus for twenty minutes twice a day; for three days following we were "checked", partly to add a bit of theory, chiefly to root out any ambitions to try harder, and were then turned loose.

The sense of going soft within is not hallucinatory. Metabolic and other changes during meditation have been measured, and all—oxygen intake, cardiac output, lactate in the blood, skin responses, brain wave patterns, recall, reaction times, perceptual-motor performance—are said to differ significantly and for the better from those in waking, sleeping, and dreaming. And of course there is a startling drop in drug use, which the movement does not emphasize because it sees itself not as a drug therapy, but as a world society with a technique and a philosophy.

The technique is for action; the philosophy I was to come to later. Its simplest tenet is "rest and activity"—as in walking the foot at rest supports the foot in movement, so the meditation supports the day's activity. The deep rest it offers is intended to "purify" the nervous system of its hoard of stresses which impede the natural flow of creative energy; unimpeded, it delivers up to us a happier assortment of thoughts, words, and deeds. Which enables us to transcend suffering and, as Maharishi said in a debatable moment, "win the game of life".

Having been baptized into a church which sees this world as a vale of tears, a few shed by me, I was to find the unrelenting optimism of meditators at times a bit more like cake icing than breadcrumbs. And when a month later I stood in the Alhambra I saw another icing, the curlicues of script carved repetitously on white wall after wall to greet the Sultan home from some military triumph and keep him modest, "There is no victor but Allah"—a grimmer view of the matter. Weltschmerz apart, however, the young folk so radiant with "purification" in this southwest corner of Spain, among them a son of mine, were six hundred arguments in favor of gratitude.

And thought.

5

Purification, a drama of internal conflict, in two scenes.

Scene one is in the lecture hall, its wooden chairs are filling up, and as they wait two young men are handling a bath sponge:

"Bought it in the co-op."

"Hmm."

"Better'n what you usually find."

"Coarser, isn't it."

"Right. Gets all those dead cells off your skin."

Curtain.

Scene two is in the co-op; this new family is sightseeing with their younger son who owns the only long hair and beard in town, except Maharishi's, and a girl sighs:

"Gee, it's good to see a freak again!"

Curtain.

6

The winter courses of what is called Maharishi International University—a learning process which takes place in the environs of Maharishi himself, pending the acquisition of other locations—were being held in a depopulated sea resort, La Antilla, about three hours by car from Seville.

We had been in three cities en route, Madrid, Seville, and Huelva, which convinced me the trip was a sizeable error. Of Madrid I saw only the men's room at the airport, where while urinating I found a pair of women with mops around my feet, a first; of Seville however I saw a lot, much of it more than once, from a rented car in which I was pursuing our lost luggage around town. There is something about luggage and the Spanish language which is basically incompatible. As for cities, their charms are much the same everywhere, from the snarlings of autos and pedestrians at their center to the spewings of factory chimneys in their outskirts, and I wake up sullen in them, like the beasts in their zoos, to go sightseeing in two thousand years of human drek. When the world-famous Street of the Serpents turned out to be a shopping arcade featuring women's shoes, I succeeded in getting my wife and son out of bed, hotel, and city, and down to the sea.

The minute I saw it I breathed again. Apart from a cluster of new high-rise apartments with a few stores in their bottoms, La Antilla was a strip of two hundred or so villas set down along the ocean for a mile, all white-plastered and roofed in red tile, low and modest, and deserted for the winter; with not more than three autos in sight, the streets were over-blown with sand, and the white town dozed in the sun as quiet as meditation itself. The only sound was the huff of the breaking sea, for miles in either direction along a beach as unspoiled as when the Phoenicians walked it.

It was these villas and apartments, their owners back in the cities, that MIU had rented for the winter as dorms; the staff had taken over a small hotel —in which Maharishi occupied a single—and converted portions into offices, co-op store, and lecture hall. Somewhere, not there, was our older son. We were cruising one of the three streets in search of the housing office when a smiling young man hailed us, and was him; we had not seen him smile like that for three years. So, what with beach and smile, that afternoon a local realtor rented the rest of us a boarded-up villa. It was dark inside, its street level a dank basement, but its second floor sprang into sunny life with a great window and a verandah and the sea for a front yard, complete with brilliant sunsets, at twenty-eight dollars a week; and there we sat and did our sightseeing, instead of touring the hotels of Spain at twenty-eight dollars a day.

I was content to spend the rest of my years in that barren villa. The winter light, too thin for swimming, was ideal for basking, and the verandah was in the sun's eye from dawn at nine till sunset at six-thirty; the three of us lived in deck chairs out there, reading, meditating, writing. I had some work in my lap that I had brought along to idle over. We ate simply, soups, cheese, sardines, but with a long chewy bread available at the grocery and excellent wines at thirty cents the half-bottle, each meal was a feast. Our older boy completed the family to take hot milk and honey with us before bedtime, after which we slept with the sea breaking up all night long at our front door.

The beach was never populous. At low tide each day it grew enormously wide, like those beaches with melting watches in surrealist painting, taken from it perhaps; and over its puddled flats I would once a day run a mile or two in tennis shorts, bare-foot. After all, a man in his late fifties, with his hair falling out, teeth falling out, and no recent testicle count, naturally likes to keep fit. But I would first walk until I was near the primitive beach beyond the last villas, where I could not be seen by medi-tators. There was never more than a score of them out along the sea—the other hundreds were shut up in their rooms over studies and meditations—but these, scattered here and there on the expanse of rippled sand, a few as couples hand in hand but most of them solitary, standing immobile or wander-ing with eyes down in thought, drifted by each other as unacknowledged as sleepwalkers, surrealist figures themselves in a painting of the edge of eternity. I was embarrassed to be seen running by them, I felt it was extremely vulgar.

7

"Maharishi's against running," says my older boy, meaning on these courses where the metabolism is to be kept low, "but he says walking's all right."

"Well," I say, interested in my daily half a loaf of chewy bread with butter, "I run to not get fat."

"If you don't want to get fat Maharishi says don't eat so much."

Maharishi is a title which means "great seer", clearly one who does not think half a loaf is better than none, and it is unquestioned by all that he is in a state of consciousness different from ours, called cosmic. Later I will learn of subtler levels, and their technical differentiation; at present I only know that I'm intrigued and skeptical. Obviously, his words, from whatever level, are taken as revelation. I hear them constantly in everyone's mouth; I can't pass two students chatting in the street without hearing his name once, and if I pass four it becomes a fugue.

"Maharishi says—"

"—in this tape Maharishi makes the point—"

"—what Maharishi says—"

"—want to be there when Maharishi's there and—"

"—as Maharishi says."

So with his photograph, it livens every bedroom in the town. The co-op, which sells stamps, toothpaste, dresses, stationery, candies, medicines, ice cream, trinkets, soaps, has a couple of tables piled with picked-over glossies of Maharishi taken from all angles, laughing or pensive, mostly in color, and black-and-whites in sizes up to a yard square; intermingled are some of a Moses-like head with extraordinary eyes, his dead master called Guru Dev, whose portrait oversees every meeting and puja. The tables are always surrounded by students, choosing. I see that these two faces inspire, bless, strengthen, and in my son's villa they look down on his housemates and him from the doors and bureaus and walls; when I walk to the grocery I pass Maharishi's picture in half the store windows, like election time.

But he himself remains invisible, to us, except on our ferry ride to nowhere. The night lectures he gives are open only to the students, who are checked at the door for identity-badges with their own photos in color, signed. Our official excuse for being in the town is to attend a symposium of guest speakers announced for the holidays; now, for lack of guest speakers, it is said to be off, and the question is whether we can get admittance to at least a lecture or two. My wife, who is very talented in human relations, disappears for the afternoon, and turns up at sunset with a pass for each of us. She has been with Maharishi, in his bedroom.

It wasn't tete-a-tete, Maharishi is not only celibate

but surrounded by a staff of twenty or so, and my wife describes their afternoon conference. In his single bedroom the staff sat on the floor and leaned against walls and stood in doorways, with Maharishi cross-legged on his bed—I say, "That doesn't sound like he's wallowing in all the money"—while he and they talked through a variety of matters, the university's architecture-to-be, a presentation for funding to British Columbia, his translation of the Vedas in progress, in the flow of which he also conducted international business on the phone with Buenos Aires and invited my wife to speak at the symposium.

I say, "Does he seem *different* from us?"

She says after thinking, "No, but very able. So many things at once, I won't tell you who he made me think of."

"Who?"

She tells me, she means don't tell anyone else; it's a famous enough producer who lives in such a brilliant maelstrom of transactions that when we first met him his convertible was equipped with two phones, one for his chauffeur.

I say, "Do you think *he's* in cosmic consciousness?"

I mean, I meditate the way I write a poem, for its own sake; I like the experience, it reinvigorates me, and its function ends there. But the young meditators I listen to see cosmic consciousness as the pot of gold at the end of the ride, my son has read me a yogi's description of its radiant blisses, and their only question is when do they open their eyes in it. To me it is a riddle, terra incognita. Unmistakably, what congregates these hundreds of meditators from a dozen countries into a community is the mind of Maharishi himself, and it is becoming for me the mystery which overhangs all the villas and their occupants. Is it really in an exalted state utterly beyond my experience and understanding?

Skunk number three, the one I genuinely want to bag.

8

My remark about wallowing in the money has a brief history.

I've never been at a lecture on meditation without hearing one or more listeners attack the initiation fee as a get-rich-quick scheme; money is what idealists are most suspicious about, especially when they want more, and Maharishi has not escaped their darkest thoughts. With this in the background, my wife and I prior to our flight had been talking over our pleasure in the technique itself and its happy effects on thousands in our son's generation.

I said, "If Tom came home tomorrow and said he found out Maharishi is stealing all the money, you know what I'd do?"

"What?"

"I'd keep on meditating."

My wife left the room, and I thought the conversation was over, but she came back.

She said, "If I found out Maharishi was stealing all the money, you know what I'd do?"

"What?"

"I'd keep quiet about it."

I have no further news on the subject, this is not

a financial report. The budget of the movement, which must indeed run in the millions, is a secret from me. As far as I could see, Maharishi owns two sheets.

9

Now with our passes in hand—not to speak of our rise in status, while my wife weighed Maharishi's invitation to speak—we had entry into the world of the students, whom we saw busy from dawn till midnight at two activities, learning and eating.

Cafeteria style, the eating took place in a kind of ballroom in the cluster of high-rise apartments a few streets back from the beach. Here on a steel counter and two long tables was a perspective of varied foods, now and then fish or chicken—I saw no meat for five weeks, and didn't notice—but always vats of soup and platters with omelette loaves or cheese slices, butter in a couple of ten-pound ingots to accompany the two great sacks of rolls, whole wheat and white, and a score of bowls with hot vegetables, salads, rice, raw bean sprouts, hard-boiled eggs, olives, yogurt, wheat germ, figs, brown sugar, honey, marmalade, and pitchers of milk ladled from knee-high cans, quart bottles of fruit juices by the dozens, wholesale cartons of cookies and tubs of ice cream, instant cocoa and coffee and packets of herb teas beside steaming kettles, and on the floor a few crates of oranges, apples, bananas, and tangerines. It was the best mass-feeding I had ever sat down to.

The students would load up their plates—their behavior on lines was unhurried, I felt my own movements as abrupt—and bear them off in quest of empty chairs. Settled, many of them sat at their untouched plates with eyes closed, saying grace. They ate at ten long tables improvised from short ones in the ballroom, where all was a babble, or out back in the sunlight of a grassy playground around a drained swimming-pool, a more tranquil tableau, or up one stairflight in the monastic hush of a mess-hall where signs on the walls said silence was precious. Done eating, they scraped and sorted their dirty ware into plastic buckets near the door, and left for their villas with armfuls of oranges and cookies and fruit juices to see them through the famine till the next meal.

"Maharishi says to a few meditators go set up a dining-room for a thousand people, and it gets done," said one of them.

It was over the eating that we mostly saw our older son, and sounded him out on his mother's speaking. This was, after all, his world we were in; it was one thing to visit it as his converts, and another to pre-empt it from the platform. It seemed our scruples were obsolete, the idea pleased him and he urged her to do it. The smile was deeper than his lips; in the silent dining-room his brother scribbled on a paper napkin, asking where I was, and he scribbled back:

27

"He's off playing golf with Maharishi."

Away from meals he was more or less incommunicado, learning. The learning took place in small-group meetings and solitary study, in the daily "rounds" of meditating, and in the lectures that called the whole community together each night without fail. The students had one day off a week, Thursday, which was a day of silence; our son spent it in studying further.

The small-group and solitary studies were, I gathered, a matter of memorizing a great deal of text—the introductory lectures, the interviews and initiations, the selection of mantras, the saying of the puja, the "three-day checking" notes to steer initiates on the path—much if not all of it in Maharishi's words; keeping to them was the way to pass on the "purity of the teaching". After my first glimpse of initiators lecturing I had said they all seemed bleached out, and I understood now it was the absence of idiosyncratic speech I felt. The puja itself of course was in Sanskrit—young folk from middle-class America who had abandoned their education because it was not "relevant" were now enthusiastically memorizing Sanskrit. Such rote was no doubt in the mouths of at least a few of the mute walkers whom I saw along the tide; more than one sat there in the sand with a notebook on his knees, learning by heart, a true enough phrase. At a lecture where my son was using a ten-minute wait to pore over his notebook, I said:

"You're working much harder here with pleasure

than you ever did at school with pain."

"Well," he said, "I feel I'm really accomplishing something."

So I looked upon him and saw myself at exactly his age, when late at night, three years before my father's death awakened me to life, I sat under the lampshade at the dining-room table in my parents' home and pored over the pamphlets of Marx, Engels, Lenin, making my notes for streetcorner orations, fortifying my head with the knowledge which would be the world's salvation, as it was mine.

Skunk number four.

The parallel would have seemed inexact to my son; it ignored "the technique", meditation, which altered the learner himself. The promise was of— by daily increments—a body free from stress and a mind open to boundless energy, intelligence, creativity, "skill in action", and "better behavior" to others. To be so altered, in some measure, was prerequisite to becoming a worthy initiator. It was this "evolution", via rounding, which all of the students were after; rounding was what they had come from half the countries of the western hemisphere for, and they cheered when the next cycle of it was announced.

One, hearing I was some kind of a writer, said impetuously, "Why don't you stay for some rounding and write something really creative?"

A round consisted of twenty minutes of meditation, five of pranayama or breathing through alternate nostrils, ten of asanas or body stretching, five more of pranayama, then once again the twenty of meditation; a dozen rounds a day meant eight or nine hours in solitude, most of them with the eyes closed. Sunrise to sunset, this inward gaze went on for weeks. It was purification on a crash program, an express ride toward cosmic consciousness, and it had its hazards. I was to see one instance of freak-out, called "unstressing", and hear that the year before when rounding was unlimited it had bred too many for comfort; now the students "went up" by one round a day, were held at twelve for a couple of weeks, and "came down" by one a day. During the cycle, they had to sign in daily at the dining-hall, a safety check.

To round was possible only in a bedroom ample enough to floor a blanket in for the body stretch-ing, and quiet through the day—I myself knew how in the depths of meditation a dog's bark could shat-ter the nerves. After Maharishi, one's past or present or future room was the obsessive topic in street chats, and the invariable question was, "Is it quiet?" In my son's villa, three good bedrooms opened off a common room, and the occupants tiptoed bare-foot past each other's doors; even so, hinges creaked, the toilet flushed, and everyone's evolution went down the drain. In other villas like ours, where bed-rooms were narrow cells with bunks, or roommates doubled up or slept on sofas, rounding was heard of, but only. And in the cluster of high-rise apart-ments, construction with derricks and drills was sporadically in progress. So there was a restless flow of students moving out and in, via the housing office on the third floor of a high-rise where, although I had business with it twice, I ran out of my hour before the queue up the staircase budged; I never saw its door.

But this flow was an undertide, minor. Day after day, in the mile strip of villas along the sea everything was motionless in the sun, the sand between the white walls was deserted, the doors were shut, and inside, in the silence of hundreds of bedrooms, were the immobile figures of meditators seated in solitude with eyes closed, evolving. No wonder at first encounter I thought the town dozed.

Of the changes in mind and body experienced in this rigor of isolation—I sampled it for a week—I am hardly qualified to speak. Certainly the slackening of the metabolism, felt in brief meditation, becomes chronic; isolation in mice and monkeys is being studied for biochemical changes in the brain, which do occur. I suspect shifts in the psyche may be as appreciable. The students' faith in them was even a bit alarmist; rounding was viewed as too potent to be done safely at home or anywhere except in a retreat like this, where one nested into a community with all needs met, no distractions, and over every head the umbrella of Maharishi's mind.

In person, Maharishi coped with all questions at the nightly lectures which brought everybody out of the woodwork into the fellowship of life; and it was these we were now permitted to attend.

10

The charm of Maharishi's umbrella is not limited to the young; I listen to the testimony of three women, fiftyish, come to new life under it.

The first is a mother I remember from a nervous chat at the airport months earlier in New York when we saw our son off; here she hails me eagerly and says I'll never guess what's happened to her, she's a "one oh eight!" The hundred and eight are a group of star volunteers around Maharishi such as in the theatre are called gophers, they gopher this and that. But it's a friend of hers who tells me what really happened to her:

"Her husband died, she was very broken up, but she started meditating and came here, and now she has a new man in her life."

"Oh?" I say with interest. "Who?"

"Maharishi."

The second, who has that soft resonance of culture found in old-world women, was initiated a dozen years ago when Maharishi first came out of India and "nobody understood a word of what he was saying", no youth around him then, only "a few sick and suffering people" like herself, with a spine in pain for years until she began meditating—

"I said, where is my pain?"—and ever since she has worked for and been in attendance on him in Europe, India, South America. She says with a slight smile somewhere between irony and simplicity:

"I spend all my money coming to these courses."

The third is a spic-and-span housewife I also first saw at the airport, where she said brightly, "Isn't it good we listen to our children?" She is from a family of thirteen meditators which will comprise four generations as soon as her first grandchild is born in a coming month and initiated, and another daughter is due here for a second course, and a son for a third; her husband is alone in the midwest, working, meditating, and paying the bills. She says:

"Maharishi is the only man I'd ever leave my husband for."

That it is a youth movement now is, it seems, a twist of history, an unforeseen meeting of a message and a generation. I ask one of them why this turn to Indian thought, why not Judaism or Christianity, and he says:

"Well, you have these freaky experiences on acid and you want to know more, who else had them, is it in a book anywhere, and who's going to tell you, some minister? but a friend says yoga is about things like that, and pretty soon you don't know anybody isn't into it."

It was this open mouth of hunger for the spiritual that Maharishi walked into, and it made of him a youth leader. What he made of them is a multitude which simply looks reclaimed, physically different from the young I see at the hamburger stands in my county, on whom there is such a look of cultural blight.

And whatever font of salvation is here, it's no tidal pool in a rock; what is breaking over the west is something of a tidal wave, like communism in the thirties, moving through the minds—by no means the shallowest—of this generation. It has lifted Jesus himself back into the pantheon. The "guru business" is alive in every city, a swarm of them—even as I am sizing up Maharishi a celebrated anti-war leader is meeting a boy guru of sixteen, and three months later tells a newspaper, "I would cross the planet on my hands and knees to kiss his feet." Our students have an impolite term for his school—"bliss ninnies"—but the competition poses a problem in manners: they ask Maharishi what their attitude should be to "other systems".

"Friendly, friendly," says Maharishi, "just point out they are a waste of time."

His own disciples now throughout the world are meditating with his technique by the hundreds of thousands; and all here will leave as new teachers of it, a crusade. In a unanimous hope of cosmic consciousness they have come from many lands—France, Turkey, Australia, Sweden, Canada, Ireland, Costa Rica, Holland, Greece, Denmark, England, Germany—and serve each other as translators; but four out of five are Americans, including a couple from a trailer in Alaska.

And, of course, one from my house.

II

So my eye was more than idly curious on the guru who one of my sons thought was "as evolved as a man can be", and the other said seemed like a "nice feller"; I was after some truth between, and nightly for the week remaining to us I watched him tend his flock in the lecture hall.

This long room—in summer, the hotel's dining-hall—had been converted into something like a theatre in the three-quarters round; a platform was centered against a wall, and around its three sides hundreds of wooden chairs were jammed. By a quarter to nine this hall was overflowing with students, some even seated in its open windows. The first row was reserved for the international staff, and directly behind them a video camera was erected. On the platform sat a divan, sheeted, and overseen by a portrait of Guru Dev; in front of it was a coffee-table with a microphone. To one side, rear, a stand was prepared for a puja. Clipped along a high wire beside it was a sheet of gauze, taped to the ceiling, which when dropped served as a transparent movie-screen visible from both sides, but edgewise to the center rows. Two pillars

in the way of a few seats bore on each flank a sign
in giant letters

H	**H**
O	**O**
P	**P**
E	**E**

for those behind them who could see little else.

"We will have a better hall soon," Maharishi
said in it during the symposium, not unwistfully.

A patio separated the hall from the hotel proper,
and the instant Maharishi and his small entourage
set foot in the patio it was known in the hall by
the communal haste to stand. Mute and moveless,
all waited with hands palmed in respect, a flower
in many of them—bought in a confectionery shop
in town, unexpectedly become a floral gold-mine
—and it took Maharishi fifteen minutes to receive
these, flower by flower, in the patio and up the
aisle and on the platform itself, around which the
students crowded. On our first night our older son
succeeded in delivering his. In time, when a woman
urged one on me to give, I understood the wish:
with each flower Maharishi met the giver's eyes,
smiled, and murmured, "Jai Guru Dev"—the greet-
ing of the movement, a kind of thanks to the holy
teacher—and the eye-to-eye contact sparked even
me.

Seated cross-legged on the divan, Maharishi
would retain a flower from his heap on the coffee-
table and, fondling it throughout, open the lec-

ture. It was really a meeting. Sometimes he had news to report, or a thought to explore and teach; more often students took a floor mike and asked questions, which ranged from uncertainties about the laundry schedule to the subtlest discriminations between the higher states of consciousness. Maharishi's answers were always sensible and exhaustive, and all bore on the conduct of life. A young man said he was "making some plans for dynamic activity", would the loss in energy retard his evolution? Maharishi said everything was a question of "priorities", and delineated most of his priorities for living. Another asked why the boat ride under "a full moon"; Maharishi said—patiently, I thought —because we believed in "fullness of life", both in the seen world and the unseen. Another said, "Maharishi, since Guru Dev has sent us such a beautiful disciple, would you tell us more about his life?" In the most abstract terms Maharishi then discoursed for an hour on the wisdom of immersion in the unmanifest for the enrichment of the manifest, concluding, with a smile that shook his shoulders, "And that is the story of Guru Dev's life." Repetitive, sometimes platitudinous, never brilliant or epigrammatic, his talk was impressive rather in its sense of large form: half an hour into one of his improvisations we were in such a tangle of digressions I saw he had lost the point—I muttered to my wife, "I don't know where he's going, do you?"—and was only meandering, but I was wrong, fifteen minutes later he began to recapitulate it all, brought it together, and came out with a complete essay. Time and again he turned his attention to the flower in his hand, caressing it as he explained about the unmanifest sap, the absolute, and its manifestations in stem, leaf, petal, the relative. It was the perennial analogy of the philosophy he was teaching, which I was to hear a hundred times. I thought a serious gardener might have grumbled at some of his views; but when he spoke of the mind's experience in the transcendental, pausing, reaching in himself for exact words, they rose with a ring of autobiographical detail, I felt I was not listening to fiction.

I next muttered to my wife, "He's not a phony."

Yet neither could I connect it with anything in me.

We sat in topcoats and blankets because the windows were open, at Maharishi's wish; a student said it was to spare him the load of our karma and sorrow in the hall. I noted more crassly that he sat baked in floodlights, and throughout his talking the camera night after night was photographing him. For years, every word uttered by him in public had been put on tape, audio to start with, now video as well, and an enormous library of his living speech was being added to daily. I was already familiar with the use made of it: weekly at "advanced" meetings in our county the audiotapes were played, and at "residence courses"—sleep-ins at country hotels, which featured three days of rounding—the videotapes took Maharishi's place at evenings like these; this teacher from a Himalayan cave was using the technology of the west to multiply his presence a thousandfold. Even here, the tapes were listened to by daytime groups, taking notes, and on two evenings when Maharishi was delayed he was seen instead lecturing at Houston and touring South America.

In close-up on the screen his broad face—or as much of it as was visible among hanging hair and beard—should have been readable; it was not, to me. His lips were full, and now and then his tongue came out to moisten them as he spoke, but no tension around his mouth was expressive of anything I recognized as individuation. Poised for speech, it changed only when he laughed, closing his eyes and heaving a little. The eyes were heavy-lidded and dark, and in his silences between phrases they worked from side to side in a way which might have been wary, but no narrowing of lids said so; they were as self-unconscious as an animal's, and opaque. I was to watch that face onscreen for hours, inscrutable, the only moods I saw on it were repose and amusement.

The meeting rarely dispersed before midnight. It was a long sit for us, yet the students loved to listen as much as Maharishi loved to talk, and once when he stirred to end it earlier a groan went up for more, more. One night he asked, "Shall we have the pundits?" and was cheered, and a few minutes later a quartet of brown-skinned men in white dhotis trouped in from the patio and took their places flanking Maharishi on the platform; two clean-shaven young uns, a middle-aged third, and a bald old man with a beard, these were the chanters from the ferry ride. What they were pundits of was the Vedas. The hall grew quiet, Maharishi murmured a word, and they commenced to recite Sanskrit in a sing-song around a chromatic drop of three half-tones, with departures into some quarter-tones, possibly intended, and I said to myself I was really in high-class clover, where else would I hear the authentic stuff? For five minutes it was eerily beautiful; it went on for ten, then Maharishi murmured for another selection, then another, and half an hour later I said to myself a lot of Sanskrit goes a short ways. It was not a concensus, the hall was rapt.

And it was nothing yet, the pundits knew every word of the Vedas by heart, as I was very soon to learn. Next time we had with us a house guest, a non-meditator, whom we were permitted to squeeze in for a treat; Maharishi sent for the pundits to illustrate his thesis that the sounds of Sanskrit embodied the physical forms of the objects it referred to—poetry, in short—and for hours he called affectionately for chant after chant which it seemed to me exhausted all the sacred books of India; when we tottered out it was after one in the morning, and our guest was livid with Sanskrit.

Our younger son said, judiciously, "Maharishi has gone too far again."

This night was the opening of the symposium,

an MIU custom—others had featured Buckminster Fuller, Hans Selye, Marshall McLuhan—which even in this obscure corner of the world provided four evenings of excellent talk by six guests. They spoke into a floor mike below the platform where Maharishi sat cross-legged and impassive, eyes closed as if asleep; but it was his commentary on each speech, always gracious, which the students awaited as its completion. A linguistics professor from MIT sketched the nature of his field—the occasion for the Sanskrit concert; a doctor from Costa Rica working in an American lab reported on brain physiology and his experiments with stress in mice —Maharishi interrupted to ask whether one finding might account for the faster reaction-time in meditation, and the doctor said yes, he hadn't thought of that; a frau professor from Germany surveyed the lifework of the Spanish poet of the region, Ramon Jimenez—Maharishi called him and every poet "fortunate", singers of "the song of the universe". The New York engineer of the world's tallest building offered an anatomy of its construction history in color-slides, with wild humor, and a professor of literature from London scanned existentialism in the novel, with subtle wit. My wife spoke on creativity and the life-cycle, and so well that next day people stopped her on the street to thank her; Maharishi said simply, "You have spoken for me," and invited her to take the floor again the night following.

When he twitched his shawl an inch higher on

one shoulder, the meeting was over; everyone rose, the floodlights went dark, and Maharishi turned to the stand to lead the hundreds in a puja by candlelight. Softly chanted by all, its culmination was a mass kneeling, a moment of silence, and a whispered, "Jai Guru Dev." Rising, Maharishi and his entourage made their serene way out to the patio, and disappeared into the hotel proper.

Leaving with my older boy another way, I said, "I think I'm beginning to fall for your leader."

"That's a kind of a typical reaction," said my son, pleased.

"Oh?" I said, not pleased. "Well, I like what he says."

"Like what?"

"Like keep your eye upon the doughnut and not upon the hole."

Actually that night Maharishi had caressed a flower and said, "When we buy the rose, we pay for the thorn; we can respond to the thorn, or we can respond to the flower." It was characteristic, and if I had to boil down to three words the hundred thousand I heard him teach that week my three would be, to love life. I am partial to the idea, thorns included.

In the absence of revelation, a society looks for its spiritual directives to whatever high priests it can find, and in ours they have been that scrambling lot we call the intellectuals. In the span of my life—modern times, from their genesis in the war just before one seer wrote *The Wasteland* and through the collapse of the Marxist hope and to our doorstep of doomsday on which another wrote *Waiting for Godot*—the counsel of our best minds has been one of despair, impotence, and self-loathing; it is the underside of the spiritual chutzpah of the Enlightenment, and it judges a century of human power and vileness without precedent. Nevertheless, I despise the counsel. What I relished in Maharishi was that he taught as though not a word of it existed, his counsel was of joy. I had expected a renunciation of the difficult world as illusion. Instead I saw in him the zest of a three-year-old for everything his thought could reach, the world was all dawn, from the rose in his fingers to his vision beyond galactic space; his favorite epithet was "beautiful", and it ran on the tongues of his followers like music, or perhaps a prayer; over and over, his teaching was to affirm their lives, augment their powers, believe in themselves. And what I relished in them was the witness of a generation which refused to accept despair as their legacy.

On the other hand, there was a price-tag on the refusal, which they were happy to pay and I was not, but at that bill I had no close look until the new year.

Late one night I went back to the dark hall, after a glove my wife had lost. It was almost two o'clock, Maharishi was still on the divan, and some other kind of session was in progress, much more inti-

mate; the rows of wooden chairs were half empty
now, and a couple of hundred students were scattered in comfort, legs outstretched. They kept call-
ing out at him, with their voices overlapping:

"—to end the generation gap."

"Maharishi, the generation gap no longer exists!"

"How about the bitterness between generations—"

I sat down in a back row to listen, and soon
enough understood what was up. The staff had in
preparation a three-day statement of the movement's goals, in films and text, to be presented the
following week to a provincial government in Canada for funding in its schools; now Maharishi was
submitting pieces of the text to the students for
rewrites. I sat there for an hour, a bit incredulous,
while a committee of two hundred amateurs strug-
gled to rewrite two sentences. But then I saw the
rewrite was not the point, the disciples were in-
structing the master. They told him what the political antagonisms in Canada were, and what was
"phony" in the films, and what high school kids
were really like; Maharishi listened, asked questions, made a few jokes. The young man I had settled next to, a housemate of my son's, sighed con-
tentedly:

"Late at night like this is the best time with Maharishi, he's just like a friend."

It was three o'clock when they broke up, and I
searched among the chairs between the pillars that
held the promise of

H   **H**
O   **O**
P   **P**
E   **E**

but did not include my wife's glove, and without it I walked back to our villa under Orion tilted over the sea, and thought of the dead teacher who once laid his finger on my soul; in every lucky life there is one, and for the hundreds of souls evolving along this winter beach I had no doubt who he was.

12

Plodding at noon on the unsteady sands between villas I cross paths with one of the symposium guests and he keeps me company in the direction of the dining-hall; he asks me how I'm liking things.

"Oh, great," I say—it's true, I'm in a glow here—"but it startles me how much abdication of self there is in these kids."

"What do you mean?"

"To Maharishi. It's like there's one heart in the whole works, his, up on the third floor, pumping the blood out to everybody else's veins."

He laughs and says, "You've never been around a charismatic leader before?"

"Charismatic leader?" I say, and it dawns on me that Maharishi is a charismatic leader. "No, have you?"

"Once. It was different in certain ways, but basically very similar."

"Who was it?"

"Castro. I was there soon after the revolution."

Castro! I mean, that's the other side of the moon, revolution, how do I figure that one out? and in

46

the trodden sands far behind my sneakers I see
another pawprint of skunk number four, the Marxist hope.

13

Next day, which was the last of the year, my wife departed for home minus her glove and me. It was not our original intention, but for reasons which will soon become unclear I signed on as a student. My wife took away with her instead the rented car, and our younger son.

I will now relieve myself on the subject of the car.

I am the efficient member of our family, which isn't saying much, but after decades of frenzy I announced I was sick of being the Genghis Khan of our caravan and was retiring; thereafter the task of herding us places devolved upon whoever cared, not me, and by what must have been luck we survived. It was thus in an otherworldly innocence that I took the wheel of our car in Seville. Too modest for comfort, a maroon American compact with a stick shift, it had been snared for us weeks ago in a web of conspiracy spun by my wife, housekeeper, and bank, all of whom have more money than I, bon-vivants together, and what I did not know was that with gas and insurance it was costing more than a dollar an hour; the company was trying harder. I did notice they took away four-fifths of my travellers checks as a deposit—the credit-card of the bank was not honored by the company it had chosen to do business with—but I expected most of it back, ha. I drove the car from the airport into the cellar of a hotel where it sat for twenty-four hours, sleeping away more pesetas downstairs than I was being charged in bed upstairs, and likewise again en route to the sea, and there in the deserted town it sat downstreet from the sand blown around our villa. It was the ugliest thing in view, and we were paying thirty-three dollars a day to look at it.

But I have learned from my fellow-meditators to be affirmative, so I will list its advantages.

First, you travel at your own convenience. Since I was now without money, I had to devote an afternoon to a trip back to Huelva, where I located a bank versed in international chores and arranged with it to receive a cable from a New York bank, after which I drove back to the realtor's office in La Antilla and phoned a friend in New York to have a bank there cable the money to Huelva, after which I waited a few days for the bank in Huelva to phone the realtor's office with word it had arrived, after which I devoted another afternoon to a trip back to Huelva to pick it up. The cash shrank in the exchange, but I don't include that or the phone call in the cost of the car, which certainly came in handy those two afternoons driving back and forth to get the money to pay for it; with no car I would have had to wait for the bus, an inconvenience.

Second, it's a time-saver. I like to save time, and it was while taking a short-cut on our second night in La Antilla that I sank it into the sand. We unloaded our belongings and portaged them under the moon to the villa; and next morning after breakfast my younger boy and I walked back with shovels to dig the car out. Over the course of an hour we dug it in a foot deeper. Throughout our shovelling, a string of meditators kept strolling past us in silence —between rounds perhaps, under orders to conserve their metabolic output—and we were accosted instead by three unenlightened Spaniards of evil face and liquorous breath who each lent a cheerful hand, and faded away before I could offer a tip. With jack and borrowed planks, we got the car backed out and drove the shovels home, in time for lunch. The walk out was ten minutes, the drive back two minutes, a saving of I would say eight minutes.

Third, it's door-to-door transportation. Well, not quite, from our door we had to trek over a storm dune which had swallowed up our fence, but once inside the car we could have driven to any door in Europe, I guess, with a new battery; the car wouldn't budge an inch. I was under instruction to phone Seville if I had any trouble, but it was a Saturday, Monday was Christmas, Sunday was Sunday, and Tuesday Seville was three hours away; also, my experience with speech in Mexico and Spain is that the citizens simply do not understand Spanish, and I had gone into telephone shock with my call to New York. So I took counsel with the realtor's office. Subsequently the car sat downstreet in the sand like a tin symbol of death-in-life while its disembodied battery travelled by hand in and out of the realtor's car to a garage in nearby Lepe—where it turned out it was also Sunday and Christmas—and the battery had a pleasant sight-seeing jaunt of four days, all door-to-door, at a cost to us of a hundred thirty-two dollars.

Fourth, it's do-it-yourself, you save the price of a driver. With me already in session as a student—in MIU's Science of Creative Intelligence, a course which staring at the car convinced me I needed— and with our younger boy's permit not valid in Spain, my wife refused to touch a stick shift even in her own language; it wasn't them, a bus would have served, but to get the goddam car itself back to Seville we had to hire a driver.

My wife was not overjoyed that I was staying, although I had warned her that once forced to Europe I might never return; it had happened before when she insisted I see the Rockies, and she repented her campaign to dislodge me again from my "rut" at home.

"Once I get out of my rut," I said, "I fly like a bird."

"Not at all," she said, "you just get into a new rut."

So I kissed the car goodbye, and their heads rode off in its rear window behind—who else?—the realtor's, bound for the Seville airport, where at the auto desk my wife suggested to the man an adjustment because of the battery and he took another fifty from her; the bill was close to five hundred dollars for eleven hours of driving, and I figured if our marriage survived this car it could survive anything, including death.

Rid of it, I will now pick up my quest of the cosmic.

14

Well, I suppose that's what I was after, and came within sniffing distance of, starting on Christmas Day.

Flashback.

The night before, the meeting had been musical and festive. Tots of some of the meditators—a couple of dozen with a few teachers constituted an MIU "prep school"—climbed the platform to sing carols for Maharishi, and among the adults who took the floor mike was a slim blond boy who moved me with two Gregorian chants; he then invited everyone to midnight mass at the local church. I hadn't known it was there.

At midnight, enough of us found our way to it that, with the winter Spaniards from a fishing settlement beyond the villas, it was standing room only in the brief white-plastered iglesia. We lingered in the rear for some minutes until the blond young meditator—someone said he was studying for the priesthood—explained the mass was to be bilingual, he would translate, and he began by leading us in carols in both tongues. But by then we were expected elsewhere, and slipped out the door.

Elsewhere was the villa next to our son's, his

small group was throwing us a party. It collected ten of us around a table with candles and camomile tea and cookies, for two hours of talk about their only topic—meditation, Maharishi, the movement—which my wife and I listened to with more than interest, we were triangulating our son's journey; and I was remembering the tea and talk of barricades in the midnight kitchens of my nineteenth year, also monoideational, the other movement which was to unnail man from his cross and didn't, but threw my wife and me into each other's eye, and so cast up on the world's beach this boy. It was a gentle and agreeable party, albeit an aging moon we walked home under.

But I had missed something in the church, and at noon through the rain of Christmas Day I went back. It was half empty for this mass, cold white, and I sat among the black garments of fishermen's widows, not knowing why I was there; I hadn't been a believer since my fourteenth year, nor heard mass since my mother's requiem a dozen years ago. I felt at home. Unexpectedly, the young meditator was again up front—on the edge of an altar ritual which had changed in my decades of absence, briefer, not in Latin, facing outward to us—and after the padre's homily he took the pulpit to give his own in English.

Speaking to what Christmas meant, he told of a nun in Calcutta who had abandoned her nunnery to care for those dying in the streets, and quoted Christ's tale of the King who said to the blessed,

Come, inherit the kingdom, for I was hungry and ye gave me meat, I was thirsty and ye gave me drink, I was a stranger and ye took me in, naked and ye clothed me, I was sick and ye visited me, I was in prison and ye came unto me, and in bewilderment the blessed said when, when? when saw we thee sick or in prison and came unto thee? and the King said, Inasmuch as ye have done it unto one of the least of these my brethren, ye have done it unto me.

I sat there with my eyes wet, not caring why, but suffused with some blessing that I felt nowhere else; I loved those rhythms as much as Maharishi his Vedas, and I had never left off reading in that mystifying book, which in its veriest nonsense somehow embodies our deepest wisdom, and on occasion with an hour to kill in a city I had wandered into some church and sat for a while, also knelt, surrendering to my childhood and mother again, for kneeling takes us down to that size, and always with this same awakening of my heart, unique to church, like some sweet plum in me that most of the time I was denying; and I thought, why? if my brain kept me from eating, and I chose to go hungry with my brain, we had thought out a poor bargain with life.

In fact, we had thought out the artist's, a pretty good one next door, but I remembered my teacher's word, sanity is to insanity as the shell is to the egg, and I decided henceforth to leave my brain at the church door, come in for the plum, and pick my brain up on the way out. In my fifty-eighth year, meditating for six months, I had never before seen I could separate myself from my thinking at a profit.

But the plum, what was the plum?

I waited outside the doors for the young medita- tor, who had a thing or two to teach me; but he was engaged with the padre after locking up the church. We exchanged names and a promise to get together. I walked home in the drizzle feeling good, some lost part of me had been found, for an hour.

I think it was the crucial item in my decision not to leave, a hunch something was here for me. Of course there was the sea and the verandah in the sun, and my older boy, and his wish that I take the month's course coming up; but my wife was going back to an empty house in the New England win- ter, with our younger off at school, and for a good part of the week I flipflopped; then I saw there were pleasant things awaiting me at home, but known, and what awaited me here was unknown. Late in the week I tracked down Maharishi's chief aide to ask might I take the course, and he said he didn't see why not.

End of flashback.

The plum was, to meet a mix of four, skunk number five.

15

I'm going to have to cook these various skunks into a delicious stew, with plum pudding, before too long; and when I do it will be in terms of the creative experience of the playwright, one skunk I know something about. For the time being, nothing much is happening—my older boy in his villa is undoing his biochemistry with rounding, I am going stoneblind in the lecture hall staring eight hours a day at videotapes of Maharishi's face, and my wife and younger boy are eloping with the realtor to Seville—and in the interim of quiet I can begin to poke around in the makings.

"He could not endure the sedentary toil of creative art, and so remained a man of action," is how one poet describes a colleague who preferred talking to writing. I quote it partly because it's a reminder that art is neither fantasy nor birdsong—the "song of the universe"—although it includes both; it is labor, of a painstaking and responsible kind. And partly because I like the little joke that all men are men of action, it's the writer who is something more, we do have our doubts.

Obviously, fantasy is not art. All are men of fantasy too, and not one of us lacks the talent to have in his dreams what he can't wrest from the world of fact. But I tell you my dream and I bore you, I tell you my play and you give me thousands of dollars; there is a difference, or there was before she rented the car. Solacing in itself, fantasy in most people is a dead end, a kind of mental onanism which procreates nothing. The mystery of art lies in why the public is willing to give the artist its money for his dreams—lavishly to the playwright, who has always been the people's artist—and the answer is not to be found solely in searching among the deprivations of the artist as the source of his art. Deprivations, like the fantasies they give birth to, are commonplace enough, and to each his own; they have no marketable value as such.

Art is means. If we are to find any clue to how it binds us together we must first look not to the artist's lacks, but to those social terms wherein and whereby his work joins him to his fellows. These terms are what we call form. It's a word which in the general means everything and nothing; I'll clarify, by a few specific examples, what it means to me.

Since we are headed—oh, much later—for the arms of that streetwalker of the literary world, the play, we might as well begin with the raw material of the medium. Pick a word. I pick a nice round one I've used several times here, "art". I no sooner write this word than a bridge, somewhat rickety in our time, springs up magically between my inner world and the reader's—more, between a choice fraction of mine and a congruent fraction of his. The word instantly does this work between us: it selects the fraction I want out of the chaotic welter of my experience, and it directs the reader in selecting out of his a fraction to match it. We meet on this bridge, and do what? build others, bridge on bridge, joining consciousness to consciousness.

Language is thus in its very nature a formal ordering of experience. It leaves much unsaid, and clearly is inexact, or I would not be defining "form" for seven paragraphs. Most of us use it semi-literately, that is, with it we manage to transact the business of the world and confuse each other. Not so—he dares hope—the writer, for reasons coming up.

Its nature as an instrument of formal ordering, while basic to esthetic—

Well, having moved from the word to the sentence, let's leave that one hanging and ponder the power of the monosyllable "while". It charges the other words around it like an electric field; it sets up in every reader's eye a tension of expectation, which demands discharge in completion. It won't get it here. The example is meant only to show how the internal ordering of language itself, in sentences, permits the creation of a certain power-relationship between speaker and listener. With this power-relationship we stand on the threshhold of esthetic form. When a literary man structures a sentence everything in it, even the punctuation, is directed at controlling the response of the reader; this semicolon differs from a period, for instance, in how it manipulates the tempo of input.

And, everything not in it. Look again at the sentence, "He could not endure the sedentary toil of creative art, and so remained a man of action." How much the poet accomplishes in it with two words, "so remained", is evident by how many I took to paraphrase it, "all men are men of action, it's the writer who is something more". The two words are more compelling than my thirteen in much the same way that, it is said, a fighter's most convincing punch travels only six inches; and this force of concentration is also part of what I mean by form.

Art is means. There is a touch of esthetic form in this sentence, it lies in the off-marriage between the singular "is" and the plural "means"; if I say instead, art is manner, a color goes out of all three words. The color is now in deviating from the expected, but a better writer has done better with this off-marriage. In *Othello*, when Desdemona disembarks, a character exclaims, "The riches of the ship is come on shore." Ignoring the variety of beauties in this sentence, which in the play are reinforced by a larger miscegenation, we see what a loss we suffer if we alter one word, "The riches of the ship have come on shore." It's the genius of the author that he knows what he can do to us with that unexpected "is"; we spy in it his instinct for good form, however rude he was to his wife.

Or consider how a later playwright outwits us, to

our pleasure, when he writes of poor Lady-So-and-So that "since her husband's death her hair has turned quite golden with grief". With a sentence built on the cliche he knows we expect, he leads us toward the cemetery and we find ourselves in the beauty parlor; this too is form.

The very sound of language is form, in English as in Sanskrit. Take two lines from a sonnet on the passing of youthful beauty—

O how shall summer's honey breath hold out
Against the wrackful siege of battering days

and hear how the writer not only delivers the ideational content—with the added reverberations of symbolic imagery; in the most sensuous way he puts it in our very ear in the texture of the sounds, shifting it from the breathing music of the first line to the shockful consonants of the second.

Here we enter another dimension of sound entirely, in the pattern of sonnet-form. The music of each word takes its syncopated place within larger musics, the five-beat line, the rhyme scheme, the fourteen lines which are given as the external profile of sonnet-form.

This water deepens as we wade in, and we have only dunked our toe. But when in our next parenthesis I mention form it should be clear I don't mean only that profile, which differentiates say the sonnet from the limerick, I mean everything in the piece, from the single unit of the word up to and including the external profile, the organization of sense, sound, image, punctuation, sentence-structure—pattern, in fine and in toto. All such elements of language and its arrangement are as much the property of the reader as of the writer; it's only because they are property held in common that the writer can use them to make his private world public. Why go to so much trouble?—it's how he gets said what the bare word leaves unsaid.

Language, which we have kept our eye to here, is only one dimension of a larger structure like the play. Clearly, the writer for a public gathered in a theatre must give formal ordering to a multitude of other elements also, most conspicuously the events of his action. The specific nature of that structure, and its relation to the private world in the playwright, is the pot in which I hope to stew these skunks.

For a while we can let them marinate. In silence, because the reason I've been staring eight hours a day at Maharishi's beard is his decree that the new year is to open with a week of silence.

16

I'm charmed by this decree, which titillates the monk in me and points to the cosmic, but it throws my course into postponement for a week; to compensate, the three days preceding silence are to be given over to a crash "overview" of the videotapes for all enrollees. In the meeting on the first night Maharishi hears the afternoon has been lost.

"Why waste time?" he says sternly, and his dark eye searches the staff in the front row; it's said he's an unsleeping taskmaster. "Who is responsible?"

Someone responsible or irresponsible explains the revised tapes were sent to Switzerland, we have only the unedited ones here, which we weren't sure he—

"But we cannot waste time," Maharishi says.

I know his view, time is the irreplaceable constituent in this world. So throughout the weekend in the lecture hall on a trio of TV sets facing three ways from the platform the unedited tapes play from ten in the morning till nine at night, interrupted only by meal times, and all day long a couple of hundred students, with a few always drifting in or out, sit among the wooden chairs basking in Maharishi's face and voice until they are glazed. I am one of them.

It's a minority of students around me, taking the course as a prerequisite to becoming initiators. Most of the students in La Antilla have already been through it in other parts of the world, as my son has, the preceding summer in California; but a few of them drop in, and so that afternoon I find him with a friend in a center row for a tape or two he wishes to reacquaint himself with, acquiring its diction like a mother tongue. It is already his, of course, in the two thick blue notebooks he has lent me—we are students together now, he the senior—which summarize each tape in detail.

I glaze easily, and a doubt I had about staying was whether I could listen to Maharishi for a month. I don't quite make it through the weekend; nine lectures on the first day, four on the second, and my brain refuses all further messages. It's not exactly a permanent loss, I will be through each of these lectures six times in the weeks ahead, and meanwhile I have a first impression.

In the tapes, thirty-three in number, about a half-hour each, Maharishi examines life from the viewpoint of Vedic philosophy; "science of creative intelligence" is his terminology, I think, for westerners. I see what the course offers is a theoretical scaffolding in which to locate the experiences of meditation itself, and a serene view of life as the unfolding of evolution, infallibly progressive, and a reconnaissance of the hiding places of creative intelligence, which I am more familiar with as the life-force. I am less familiar with the halving of the

cosmos into the absolute and the relative, pure Intelligence and its manifestations, and am relieved
that Maharishi counsels me to "enjoy 200% of life",
100% in each. One tape makes me sit up. I hear him
say something to the effect that "when Intelligence
prepares to play a role in its own field, it becomes
consciousness; when existence becomes conscious,
Intelligence becomes intelligent"—becomes, that is,
creative intelligence—and with a tingle I think but
that's Genesis. A match has been lit under my pot
of skunks, but I don't know it yet; I know only the
course smells promising, and I stagger out for a
breath of sea air.

So we come down to the last hour of the old year,
which finds me and my son side by side in the
nightly meeting; Maharishi is outlining the Canadian
presentation scheduled soon. At midnight everything is interrupted. It's the first new year I think
in thirty-six that I have not greeted with my wife;
instead I shake the hand of the young man beside
me who is flesh of our flesh.

I say, "Here's hoping you and I and Mommy and
Dan and everybody we know has a good year."

And he says—

But shall I tell the truth? for four years I've been
in mourning and not for my dead, it's for this boy,
or for whatever corner in my heart died when his
childhood slid out of my arms, and I know the moment it hit me when on a street in New York a
kindergarten class straggled past my eye with one
character in a fringed deerslayer jacket and I un-

derstood that our small sprite in the same deerslayer
jacket was nowhere, gone, never to be caught up or
ride on my shoulders again, and the dissolution of
my young fatherhood when I was indeed in height-
ened consciousness is half of what I mourn, love
before its budding of impurities, and the other half
is that for four years I've suffered to watch this
boy suffer in the poisons of his teens, going down
in eddies of self-hatred after some rock in himself
to stand on, drowning perhaps, and that is the truth,
a year ago I thought he was drowning and couldn't
catch him up to ride on my shoulders in his fringed
jacket—

And he says evenly, "I think we will."

Meanwhile Maharishi invokes a group meditation
to begin the new year. The hall goes totally dark for
five minutes of it with much giggling, leftovers of
original sin; and he next leads us in a candle-lit puja,
with no giggling; and the pundits then mount the
platform for a brief recital in Sanskrit, fifteen minutes only. So the year is baptized, in the quest of
the spirit.

The meeting resumes, with last rewrites on the
Canadian text before the silence settles in, but my
son and I with others make our way out of the hall,
and under the stars the two of us cross the sand
between the dark villas to mine, the land of hot milk
and honey, and after talking idly over it a while we
part for the night; below my kitchen window he
walks along the sandy road under one streetlight, and
is gone in the dark. I go to my bed, very content.

17

Nothing happened during silence week, that was its point.

It had rained for a couple of days, with the sea winds driving in at the slide window, puddling the floor; on such nights the villa, with its bare light-bulbs and a fainthearted heater in each bedroom, was pretty bleak. Silence week however was marvellous weather, sun uninterrupted by one cloud, and at its end two happy meditators told me, "Maharishi said don't be surprised if the sun shines." I wasn't anyway, and sat out my silence stripped, sunbathing and meditating.

"Meditate, meditate, meditate," Maharishi had directed us at the meeting, "spend all week in the transcendental."

I spent it on the verandah. And for all I know in the transcendental too, a state which I would discover was elusive, even to old hands among the students.

Dawns were late by the clock here, but by ten the sun was up out of the sea enough to warm the second-story verandah, and my day's business on it began. I sat in a deck chair, eyes closed, and the first morning and afternoon I did two meditations each, which of themselves grew from fifty minutes to about seventy-five. Or, six times more than usual. My lunch break included an hour afterwards—the metabolism of meditation contradicts that of digestion. I varied the second day by throwing in two rounds, twenty-minute meditations alternating with the pranayama and asanas my son had taught me in his villa before silence. The pranayama I did in the chair, pinching a nostril shut while I breathed without sound; the asanas I did on a blanket spread on the verandah, a set of toe touchings, shoulder stands, body twists. Although by the fourth day I was up to nine rounds—and wrote my wife, "This rounding takes up all one's time!"—the increase was in the pranayama and asanas, and the meditation itself remained at about four hours. In it the body loses the sense of its own weight, so the deck chair never grew uncomfortable; all week I sat submerged in my reveries, and the only sound of the world was the sea working so constantly it was no sound, and the sun inched from east to west across my contented eyelids. I ended my labors, to stretch a word, around six—night sessions interfere with sleep.

I don't know what goes on in the heads of other meditators; I will describe mine.

Since the mantra has no meaning, it occupies the surface of my mind without captivating the bulk, and under it my other thoughts settle into a dreamlike liquidity; they swim by as they wish, images and voices, which I make no effort to interpret. In theory, the crevice I am to experience between them and the mantra, when thinking neither, is "pure consciousness". Void of content, this is the transcendental or fourth state—after waking, sleeping, dreaming—and the mantra is a "vehicle" to take me there; dipping into the transcendental is initial to the growth of cosmic consciousness. Could be. In practice, the mantra seems like a sop I toss to my mind to outwit its need to make meaningful connections, and while it nibbles I sink below, leave behind the demands I habitually make of myself, and so am half out of the skin of personality; the sense is one of mute witnessing. To create this witness for keeps is an ultimate, but every writer knows the second man in himself of old, and the difference is that this one has no wish to publish.

Luckily, for the reveries I sat submerged in were a Humboldt Current of trivia.

"Any interesting experiences?" my son wrote in his notepad at dinner.

"Today the sea came up inside my belly," I wrote back, hoping to be interesting.

Unimpressed, he wrote, "Anything can happen in rounding."

This garrulity in the dining-room came to an end in midweek when he and his housemates decided "to go all out" by staying in; they meditated around the clock, three and four hours at a stretch, and left me to my infantilia. I ate alone then, and nightly filled a bag with oranges, crackers, cheese, nuts, yogurt, raisins, and fruit juices from a table where a sign said, "Take a bottle to your room for silence week." I took it to my son's, by his request, or at least to the table in his villa where the three bedroom doors were dumb as I tiptoed in and out. Once or twice he opened his, and we exchanged a smile and a scribble; otherwise we left notes. And in one of his I read that my countenance was "swelling with love and warmth, and many stresses are gone the last few days"—which he attributed to my rounding, and I to his.

I did feel internally clean; towards the end of the first afternoon some bleakness and a touch of anxiety had stirred in me, but faded when I opened my eyes at last. Unpleasant images left no residue, I sat for an instant at my mother's deathbed so truly that something in me gasped, it came and went. Two or three dogs yapping below me seemed actually on the verandah and around my flesh like a vicious pack, a frightening couple of minutes with my eyes closed, until they chased each other away. More pleasantly, the sea did come up into my belly the third morning; facing it, I heard its waves till they crept ashore and through my skin like a porous membrane and broke inside my belly, where I no longer heard but felt them, for a full minute the sea and I were indistinguishable, after which it ebbed out and back to its proper place. Dialogue constantly slid by, a scrap of which I remembered verbatim, someone interrogating me about a lightbulb on the ground: "Who put that bulb there?" "I did." "What for?" "It's a symbol." "Of what?" "Of my dead father's love." Most of my phantasmagoria was agreeable enough, but I treated it all like a flow of mental garbage, I was only being. At day's end I was left with a certain glumness in the mouth, from lack of use, but merely there; I felt simple, clearheaded, and benevolent.

"Silence is growing in us," said Maharishi, "and silence means harmony."

For exercise, I walked a quiet mile along the beach before dinner, among a few other meanderers; my son had cautioned me not to run, but my metabolism had no desire to, I had joined the sleepwalkers.

If the town seemed dozing before, it was now spellbound. The lecture hall, speechless for the week, was restored to its former existence; it served as an auxiliary dining-room, with bowls and trays of cold foods along its steel counter at one end, and here—only a street inland from my villa—I picked up lunch, eating on the porch or steps with a dozen others in silence. The patio between hall and hotel was posted with cautionary signs—"Maharishi's Silence Is Precious"—and at the hotel door a guard or two sat on chairs, to keep noisy feet out. Its lobby had been where the incoming mail was sorted and called for, but the rack had been moved out to a building six blocks away; the lobby was deserted. The co-op too was closed, except for an hour in the evening, when business was by pantomine under a sign reminding one and all of their proximity to "the Core of Silence".

This term I took to mean Maharishi himself, overhead, incommunicado in his single on the third floor, and I went back to my novitiate on the veran-dah, wondering what he was up to. Meditating? fast-ing? playing solitaire? no one knew. On the seventh day even his chief aide said to all of us, "If I'm per-mitted to see Maharishi—" And on the eighth when himself in his white dhoti and beads emerged to meet with us, he was weak of limb and voice; some-one offered a guess that "nothing went in or out of that body all week".

Not so mine, and in my digestive time off I scrubbed my clothes in the sink and hung them on the verandah to dry, jotted down scraps of a running letter to my wife, and cleaned house. It had passed into the hands of MIU on the first and I was no longer paying rent, but tuition, and ex-pected housemates whenever they could struggle through the spell of silence; so I stripped the double bunks in the bedroom cells, cleared out shelves in the bathroom cupboard, swept the floors of the sand I imported in my sneakers, and made the villa per-fect for whoever might come to mess up my idyll of solitude. In the evenings I read in bed, and wrote a little.

It was that, an idyllic week, I loved the silence. The rounding turned a bit tedious, but the silence sweetened me towards the people it saved me a lot of talk with, and I guessed if I remained mute I could be as sociable as anyone. It was said one boy after silence the year before had never come out; I figured if Maharishi laid a hand on his head and said speak the boy would, and I thought I'd ask my son to arrange this courtesy for me, if necessary. I was to surrender my first word with a sense of loss—of virtue, energy, wholeness.

But on the day I was aiming at ten rounds it came to my attention I wasn't supposed to be doing any of this at all; enrollees in my course were to have kept their heads normal. I tapered off over the week-end, both relieved and reluctant. The tedium was creeping in, and my skull felt "overrested", as with too much sleep; but perhaps that was itself the barrier I hadn't broken through, and whatever seventh heaven was on the third floor was still beyond me.

I came out of silence with a cosmic tan.

18

In the dining-room, silence week half done, I sit
with my breakfast tray next to a woman I recog-
nize, and take out the pen and paper my son has advised me to carry for necessary conversation; I decide what's necessary.

I scribble, "How's your room?"

"My room?" she says. "Oh—"

And she tells me—a new arrival, she's not in silence like us old-timers—that it's small, it's dirty,
she's not happy with it.

She's in her thirties, small herself. I first saw her
late at night after my wife's lecture, surrounded by
her luggage on the steps outside the hall, tired, just
in from Israel, and without sheets in some room to
sleep on; trying to be decent, she was fretful about
everything, an old war in her. I thought you come
here to be near Maharishi, you're near him, why
fret about sheets? and invited her to stay the night
with us. She hesitated, but a meditator was off trying to find her a sheet or another room; she said
she'd wait. I haven't seen her since. What she's not
happy with of course is herself; after silence we
will meet again and talk of Israel, where she lives

with a shrug, and when I ask her name she says apologetically, "It's only Miriam"—I think what did she feel I had a right to, Nefertiti?

But here and now she wants not to be fretful, it's small and dirty but she concedes at least it's a room, and she rises to a flight of affirmation:

"Things could be better."

I scribble, "They're better in heaven."

"Oh?" she says, with a touch of wryness which may rescue her, "isn't this it?"

So after a moment I scribble, " 'Why, this is hell, nor am I out of it.' "

Which neither of us understands.

I do, afterwards, thinking of course it's heaven—or hell—and so was Israel, where my wife and I drove around for three weeks in exaltation, laughing and crying every other sacred or profane minute over places, people, ideals, ancient and modern. I need never have left Kansas—where the stranger passing a farmer on a fence asks what kind of people live ahead, the farmer asks what kind were they where he's from, he says terrible, the farmer says that's the kind live here, and another stranger passes with the same question but the people where he's from were lovely, so the farmer says that's the kind live here—to learn from the Vedas that "knowledge is structured in consciousness".

Israel is another handsome skunk, like my love in young fatherhood before the impurities, but they keep coming back to me now, I've lost count. The question is not whether our lives contain exaltations, but when?—and what if anything have they to do with cosmic consciousness?

Because I see I am opening in one here.

19

Silence, albeit not voluntary, is an old story with writers; we don't call it harmony, we call it a block. But it's a door to that harmony which the writer finds in mastering his experience, and while uninterrupted in silence week we should have a look at it.

I was doubly pleased with my son's note about my "love and warmth" because I do not disagree with a great novelist who, creating a character who was also a novelist, comments, "Like most writers, he was a cold man." It is from the horse's mouth. Yet it may be an expression of writer's guilt; could one say, like most humans?

The warmth of the work means little, of course—charm, compassion, candor, all are aspects of form. I suppose the personality of the writer is met in a multitude of variations; in my own acquaintance most of us, however externally sociable, have something withheld, secretive, and wary in us. It's the witness, the second man, and it breeds some of the guilt: we suffer nothing, our own woes or others', without an eye to how it can be used. The system of thought I was soon to be lectured in inculcates this witness or some cousin of it as the dispeller of suffering, and the schizoid psychotherapists I know call it schizoid. It is notoriously self-involved, and the wives' dialogue about the playwright is classic:

"How is your husband when he's working?"

"Impossible."

"But when he's not working?"

"Worse."

At the same time, every successful playwright has the knack of seducing the public into supporting him in exchange for sharing with it certain of his experiences, peculiarly organized, so as to range from entertainment to revelation. The paradox of the artist is that he can be, and at close quarters often is, so unfeeling in his relations with his fellow citizens, and simultaneously possesses, in a measure beyond any of them, the social tact to move their hearts. Peculiarly organized means form, and I think it's only in the realm of form that the paradox is resolved.

But I prefer to leave the level of abstraction to bolder minds, and come down to that of autobiography, where I am the only authority. Here I must—

Pardon me, an interruption.

Housemates! at my door in the night. I let them in over the oddity of brick wall which fills the doorway knee-high to keep the tide out, and upstairs.

I read their slips from the housing office, two young men with German names, new arrivals; they speak little English, and I none—it's still silence—but in mime I welcome them to their cells, each with its double bunk of concrete and a wooden chair. They set down their bags, bedlinens, blankets.

Drafty and half in dark, with the wiring in the main room shorted out and a rickety table with some wooden chairs on a cold floor of clay tile, the villa is not at its best at night, is in fact hideous, so I beckon them onto the verandah to consider the grandeur of stars and sea. I then retire to bed, and write a bit. In the morning it appears they have both moved into one cell, its door shut; the other is unoccupied. Seven hours later when I tap to see if they are dead, I discover they don't live here, and never did.

Now.

I must confess that, despite my earlier talk of painstaking toil, writing when it goes well is no trouble at all, and hardly deserves the name of work. It is life's chief delight, enhances my capacity to delight in the rest of life, however commonplace, and is so indistinguishable from play that I often stop in wonder that the citizenry supplies me with food, clothing, and shelter, simply for building with my colored blocks. Which breeds a bit more of the guilt. Yet for twenty years the citizenry contributed nothing to my guilt, which in no way emptied the play of its inherent pleasure or significance for me.

I said when it goes well, because when it goes badly my experience is just the opposite. It is life's chief burden, diminishes my capacity to enjoy anything, however delectable, and is so indistinguishable from outhouse-cleaning that I often wish I'd taken that up instead—at least the material is there, given, and in full view. These spells somewhat lighten the guilt. But I know of no artist who wouldn't sell a lung to be always in the state of creative grace, and of none who does not go cyclically into that state of damnation, seemingly eternal, when he's as sterile as a stone.

This figure of speech isn't arbitrary; I feel that a process of petrifaction has overtaken my skull—it *thickens*—and some elusive organ in the region of my heart, with the result that I live through each day on approximately twenty percent of my metabolic vitality. It is not dissimilar to what I feel towards the end of this week of silent rounding—physiologically, not in mood—and perhaps if I were wired up the gauges might read the same. Yes or no, this too is "rest and activity", and no activity other than writing unlocks the remaining eighty percent of me for my use. I always know—seem to know—what it is I want to work on; if I had to submit a synopsis of a project for a grant I could get up four any day of the week, and describe each eloquently and persuasively. The only thing I can't do is write it. When I sit down to try, the living words do not come; the idea is as speechless as a manikin, and the only sound to be heard is the snoring of my eighty percent. The sense of it, says—

Pardon me.

Housemates! at my door, two in one afternoon.

The first is a man in his thirties, athletic and brisk, whose tour of inspection is brief; he stares at the double bunks, and remarks that he "couldn't have sex here". I disagree, though in silence, thinking of how rhyme often forces a poet into tight corners and unexpected openings. But the remark is unusual in our spiritual air, and I don't relish lying awake while he and his love fall out of the bunk all night; I'm not altogether sorry when he says I'll hear from him and takes off. I never do.

Writer's block, perhaps.

The sense of it, says a fellow playwright, is being "seething and swollen, like a woman fifteen months pregnant and unable to sleep or turn, crying aloud, Oh God, out, out!" In vain, it can slumber on in there for months, during which I occupy myself with moving my collection of speechless manikins around from shelf to shelf of my workroom. The one fatal tactic for me to adopt is to become a man of action and go to the movies during workhours, or turn in any other way consumer—that degenerates into an orgy of cramming fodder into my mouth, and only brings me to death's door of starvation. It's in this phase that many would-be writers escape into such lazy and cowardly professions as lion-taming and polar exploration. I myself have only one technique for ending the silence, it's to sit at my desk and survive it; I polish this manikin and I polish that manikin, and lo! the day comes when one of them opens its idiot's face and speaks.

It speaks living words which—whatever their surface content—say one thing to my moribund self, Lazarus, come forth! and my eighty percent opens one eye; sometimes he closes it again. But if what's on the desk interests him enough to open the other, rise, and settle down to serious play, I am back in business. Because the eighty percent which must awaken to work the material is itself the material to be worked—it's a chain reaction, matter into energy.

I can only guess at what's happened in this moment. The sensation is one of things, internal and external, opening up; and I understand this too in terms of form. I should mention here that I never—

Pardon me.

The second visitor is the author of a note, left in my absence at lunch, saying he'd like the cell which sleeps east for "quiet to evolve in"; now he's back to move in and not move in, a gentle boy who despite his cowboy mustache thinks he's "indecisive", not sure he prefers his present room or this one, but is sleeping in a third. To keep all choices open, he leaves a blanket on the bunk, and a bottle of Dr. Bronner's supermild-100%-natural-coconut-olive-peppermint-oils-pure-Castile-soap in the bathroom. It's the brand my son and many of the youngsters have on their shelves, two dollars a pint, indispensable to purification—its label says, "Use love, fulltruth, God's law and Bronner's Soap to clean body-mind-soul-spirit"—and why must this particular boy sleep east? because if the head lies north it's drained of psychic energy by the magnetism of the pole. I quickly in my mind run through the beds of my past life, wondering which one I went wrong in, but not all meditators observe such rules and I have no chance to explore it further with this one; overnight his blanket vanishes, and with it his soap.

Which I'm beginning to think maybe I need.

I was saying I never write first drafts. They always turn out to have been first drafts, when for the theatre, but what my hand commits to paper has nothing tentative about it; I rewrite phrase by phrase, and the completed paragraph, scene, opus, is meant to stand as a final and total formulation. Most of the time, when not for the theatre, it is. I have criteria which tell me—all of them intuitive, and some alas deceptive—when this finality in each unit is achieved: while writing I'm gazing in two directions at once, in to myself and out to an audience, and what I put down on paper must satisfy standards in both directions or it will not put down.

The standards facing out are concerned with those aspects of form I touched on earlier—logical sense, sound, image, structure—as the means of making the unit not only intelligible to the mind of whatever audience I'm aiming at, but impactful upon its physique; they are intended to assure, insofar as it lies within the writer's powers, that the audience shall not only comprehend what he said, but feel what he felt. This emotional reverberation is the sine qua non of these standards, and it requires that the writer have an unusual empathy for his audience and their responsiveness to formal shapings.

The standards facing in partake in the same aspects of form, but their sine qua non is discovery—

and here, if anyone has been waiting, we come to the idea of content. The moment of what used to be called inspiration is a moment of discovering something new and unwritten in myself. Perhaps this is why I fail in writing the projects I know I want to write; in a sense, a condition of writing is not knowing. Such discoveries come not as raw content—raw, it's everyman's fantasy, which is behind us—but with some attributes of form, and may range from a turn of phrase to the overall concept of a large piece. It's not necessary that I understand what it is I'm discovering in myself; my touchstone for the occurrence of discovery is my thoracic excitement, and the act of wording it is accompanied by an elation and a sense of liberation. I think both have to do with the freeing of something hitherto imprisoned, and the elation with—additionally—the sense of power over the anticipated audience.

But I must stress that this discovery inward, and formulation outward, happen simultaneously, or so close thereto that I can't say which has come first. My belief is it can be either, and my point is we must have both. It's as a commentator that I talk of form and of content; the creator knows only the simultaneity, in which thinking and feeling are one. So if most writers are cold men—

Pardon me.

Housemates! at my door, two on the weekend as silence ends, and, mirabile dictu, actually are moving in.

The first is a music student in one week ago from

Texas, who arrives with a powerful electric heater in hand and nothing else; his luggage has sunk out of sight beneath the Spanish language. The second is a math student in ten weeks ago from Colorado, who as soon as he views the sea from the verandah runs all the way back to the housing office before they give the room to someone else. With lost luggage and the sea in common, the three of us it turns out also are pianists; we look forward to a congenial occupancy of the villa in the weeks ahead.

So.

If most writers are cold men, is it not perhaps that they function somewhat as human iceboxes?—preserving certain of their experiences in themselves, frozen and unfelt, against that day when all the conditions for thaw luckily meet. The conditions are those of mastery. Such buried experiences arise in the writer only when he has a net of form to waken and catch them in; and it is the very net in which he catches his public. The public pays him to waken them too, and share in the mastery. Of what?—that we will come to when we look at the form the playwright works in, which will explain much.

Pending the miraculous convergence of the conditions for inner mastery, the writer is silent, and waits; he is "withheld". Others meanwhile throw themselves wholly into relationships, feelings, actions to change things around them—rooms, for instance—in an everyday attempt at outer mastery.

It is more direct, and less binding. My housemates are no sooner settled into the villa, joyous with the ritual of sea and sun on the verandah, than we are all three yanked out and banished to hotel life in a boom town with a skyline of streaming smokestacks.

20

Just before our banishment I sit at lunch listening to a dark-haired girl, not quite like the others, who will be a beauty when the sallow immobility is off her face; she can't smile, it hurts her upper lip.

She is saying, "He's very old and there's only my sister, he's built up this big shoe business, it seems funny to think soon I'll have all that money."

I say, "If you had it now, would it solve your problem?"

I don't know what her problem is; she thinks it over, whatever, and shakes her head.

"No."

"Seems totally irrelevant?"

She says without expression, "Yes."

She is banished with us next day to the hotels in the other town; I see her now and then at meals, and when my last week is up I stop for another word with her over lunch.

"Things are better with you."

She agrees with a nod. "Well, we didn't have hot water again yesterday, but—"

She doesn't know what I mean; her lip is objecting less to a smile, her skin has a hint of light coming into it, she is looking more like the others.

21

Group psychology, amateur notes on.

The housing arithmetic in La Antilla had become unsolvable with the new year, when the first batch of six hundred students was expected to leave, vacating rooms for the next batch; four hundred of them stayed. Why?—for more rounding, of course, but also for the ozone of a society made up of them and their leader. The riddle of Maharishi's state of consciousness was not amenable to my inquiry, but theirs was, and I was living more intimately with them now; I saw that in Maharishi's bosom they were happier than they had been anywhere since their expulsion from the garden of childhood, and only his exhortations to get out and save the world drove them from him. Coming and going, they said one sentence over and over:

"It's so good to see Maharishi again."

It was a sentiment which lubricated a lot of bumpy going. Leader and group, they were a huge family, a nomadic tribe pitching tent for a season in this or that spot on the globe, but unlike any family I ever had; in six weeks among them I heard literally not one sharp word. Some were spoken, no doubt. But in the terminology itself there was a blanket forgiveness of anything harsh as "unstressing", like a hiccup, gone forever. And human nature as it used to be was very little in evidence.

A girl in charge of many unmanageables, housing, food purchasing, registration, was so burdened I could get a question to her only by marching at her side in the night from one building to another; next time I greeted her:

"Hi, they still hassling you?"

She said, a smiling point of honor, "Oh, I'm never hassled."

I was insulting her; to be tense, passionate, driving—everything their money-making fathers were—would have been vulgarity.

So their gestures were legato, their voices soft, their smiles unfailing, half of which was the physiological effect of rounding; the other half was Maharishi's image in them. For he was in their bosom too, from the necktie on the outside to the ethics on the inside. Their jackets and ties, moderate hair, clean-shaven jaws, were in strict compliance with his wish—my younger boy was turned away from one meeting for lack of a tie—that they not look like freaks when proselytizing; for thirty nights I too was to wear a tie, which I had become a writer principally to escape. More inwardly, each initiator was to be an "embodiment" of the teaching, and "live the knowledge he imparts". In Maharishi's presence, I saw every follower go into a slow-down, call it humility, of hesitant limb and tongue, like a touching of even talk with the fingertips; not in his presence, the slow-down was internal. It was a state of being in love, thus the prevalence of the iconography. That I heard no sharp words was hardly an enigma—anger was weakness, said Maharishi, and the image of a charismatic leader in oneself defuses the impulses alien to it.

In brief, it was a family for the reconstruction of the psyche, and that image was potent in it. The imitation of a worthy master is the "devotional" path to enlightenment, which Maharishi was said to have pursued for thirteen years with Guru Dev; it implied a monastic rule of obedience, to the point even of anticipating the guru's least wish, until one became him; it didn't work if you picked the wrong guru. But such was the tradition for the abdication of self I had blinked at in this family.

Its structure was thus a kind of thearchy. Maharishi made all the decisions; pending each—like that on the housing problem, which waited for him to come out of silence—no one initiated a move. Once his chief aide, bringing us a third set of contradictory instructions, began on a note of willy-nilly humor:

"This is as of thirty minutes ago, I may be countermanded at any moment."

Laughter, which was habitual. In the early days, when the students around Maharishi in India numbered eighty, the problems were simple; now we were more than a thousand. So many procedures were improvisatory, and went so wildly wrong, that I said I knew why to "take it as it comes"—a phrase in teaching new meditators—was basic, it was a survival mechanism; but the groans of dismay that went up were more or less playful. And none of these snafus was serious, they meant at worst we had to stand on line again.

"Maharishi likes to confuse us," said the aide, "it keeps us on our toes."

In line. I stood on line for maybe seven hours in my first couple of weeks—for an identity badge and a tuition payment—and half the time nobody was doing business at its head, or it was other business; I estimated it averaged out to a loss of seven hundred man-hours per week, but this kind of thinking was only my vulgarity. I ran into instances of morale deflated by the snarls in procedure, but when I mentioned it to my son's housemate he went blank with incomprehension:

"Bad morale? Where?"

Well, a for instance. The immediate shortage in housing had been met by renting a piece of another town an hour's drive away—called Punta Umbria—and opening a second campus there for newcomers; rumors of complicated moves were in the air. Silence week hushed them. But instructions had been issued for some of us to move out, and at the last hour cancelled; so students who had turned in their blankets and towels went into silence week on naked mattresses with nary a sheet to dry their ears. Which added to asceticism, but not to enthusiasm for the staff.

One meditator—an army veteran who had picked

up a paperback by Maharishi in Alaska and said it was the first time God made any sense to him—quit a line muttering in disgust from his cross:

"They don't know what they're doing."

It was his judgment on the organization in toto; later he said he wanted "nothing whatever to do with it" after he left, but would just get out in the field and initiate. Not unique, this reaction too was tolerated as "unstressing", and more striking was the fact that most students outrode the calamities in joyous humor. Apart from a common view that they were planned as benefits for our evolution, one explanation of staff confusion—which I attributed to paralysis while awaiting word from above —was that Maharishi couldn't "take that load of karma from others and do what he must do"; none of the dissatisfactions rubbed off on him. But on one queue or another I questioned my fellow students on the "skill in action" the years of meditating had developed in the staff.

"Well, I figure they're from the early days with heavy druggers," said one meditator, "they just started on a pretty low level."

"The only way I can figure it," said another, "is everything below Maharishi is chaos."

Not chaos, but a staff whose amateur status grew the further down it one went, and we were at the bottom. From that worm's eye view, I gathered professionalism was confined to specialists like the doctors who ran the clinic and the plumbers, both imported from abroad.

Closest to Maharishi I imagine was his entourage of compatriots in dhotis, the two or three "brah-macharyas"—celibate disciples for life—and the pundits; there was also a young American serving as personal secretary and chauffeur. What the students called the international staff I took to be, first, the leaders from larger countries, the MIU directors, and other literate heads. These I heard were salaried, at modest amounts, but sufficient to support families; it was known that either celibacy or monogamy was what Maharishi wanted around him. Next was the administrative staff—school, finances, housing, transportation, everything—who were students up from the ranks working for board and pocket money, twenty or thirty dollars a month. Unsalaried were the hundred and eight, not necessarily their number, the figure was Vedic and mystical. This select group of volunteers accompanied Maharishi on his travels and took on a multitude of minor chores; they paid their own fares and board, and it cost each about five thousand a year, which is what made them select. The menial staff, kitchen and laundry and cleaning squads, were kids without money who worked for two ten-week sessions in exchange for free tuition at the third.

Tuition with keep cost the rest of us about ten dollars a day, and what this staff was presiding over was a winter income of a couple of million dollars. I did not doubt a managerial expert or two would have whipped the tribe into order, and saved a good bit of money, but not without creating a sour climate of "them and us"; meditators all, on a first-name basis from top to bottom, this society in its mishaps was a brotherhood, a kind of circuitry of comfort and strength. That current I guessed was second only to Maharishi's image in the work of psychic consolidation.

In the terminology it was "support by the environment", and there was no other. Tucked away on this coast, we were an island in a sea of Spanish, without newspapers or radio, so isolated from the world that in my six weeks I heard only three bits of news—Lyndon Johnson had died, a Vietnam truce was in the offing, Foreman had kayoed Frazier—and my ear was indifferent as any. I thought it was the truce an Australian meditator meant when he spoke with pleasure of "the way the news is developing the last few days"; he meant our army had given permission for initiators to lecture on bases at home. From our island, such a tie to the movement lent the outer world its reality, otherwise its news was a dream which didn't matter.

This isolation, like everything else my eye fell on here, was characteristic only of the school course, not of the movement day-to-day in the world. But I wondered whether these priestlings were nervous about stepping back into its contradictions after their months of retreat; I had my son in mind. Yes, said one, but the answer was to throw oneself into teaching, work for a local center, live with other meditators—in short, recreate what was here. This was exactly what my son would return

to do; the year coming up would be the most meaningful and comfortable of his life. It was the counsel Maharishi urged upon students, adding more
than once:

"Don't doubt the experience you have had."

The experience was of inner unification, or—
shall we say?—mastery. My own sense of the soul's
opening to benevolence was common to all in this
encampment; when I inquired, they said of course.
It was born not only of the rounding itself, in the
fusing brotherhood of leader and group, but of a
world ideology which explained the past and a
world plan which would change its future. Ideology
and plan were what I now looked forward to, on
the other side of the housing snarl.

There I was to encounter all of this in miniature.
Opening the unlocked door of my hotel room, iden-
tified by a name card, I saw my papers had been
shifted; I then realized a squad of the college girls
who drifted around in threes, hair in bandanas,
mops and pails in hand, had been in to clean up. I
found a note on the desktop—

Dear William,
              Hope the room is to your liking.
Jai Guru Dev.
              Your MIU maids,
                   Joan, Mary, Sue

On the note they had left four candies for me. I
was so enchanted by this kind of hotel service that
I at once sat down to record it in the running letter

to my wife—I began, "What a place!"—which however I could not then detach from the desktop;
while cleaning the girls had been dripping honey or
something, and my letter was stuck in their goo.

But this was after the housing arithmetic had
been solved by moving all the La Antilla students
to Punta Umbria, and all the Punta Umbria students to La Antilla.

22

"Since one of the things we are learning here is not to build permanent houses in the relative world—"

So begins the aide who on the ninth morning of the year informs us in the lecture hall that we are to be packed and ready to move out two hours hence. The procedure—"which appears ridiculous on the face of it, but is probably the best"—is for us to wait till the buses arrive with the Punta Umbria students and swap room cards with them at random. This scheme is greeted with a universal moan, and never heard of again; subsequent word of mouth leads us to report to the housing office at noon, several hundred strong.

The line starts on the third floor, winds down the two flights of stairs, and snakes out into the unpaved street among the new high-rises, where it idles for half an hour; the word is then passed to move backward until the stairs are cleared, a staggering maneuver, which breaks through a second line waiting to get into the dining room. Since I now have a choice, I decide I am on the lunch line. In the milling, a girl from the housing office makes an invisible appearance with an inaudible announcement, rumored to be that we are to turn in our room cards for bus passes. I have no room card, a consequence of my private renting of the villa; but my Colorado housemate, a born outwitter of systems, has five or six extras in his pocket, and issues me one. I sign it, and within a few minutes he slips me a bus pass.

With our Texas housemate we eat out back on chairs around the dry swimming-pool, where we are joined by a handsome lean Kentuckian, who sits cross-legged on the grass with his plate; deep in thought, he ignores our small talk.

"I've been thinking," he says in a pause, not lifting his head, "there's sixty-four chapters in the Vedas, and there's sixty-four elements in the biological table. If you take the four basic elements, one of them can be missing in any object of perception—"

"Four?" I inquire.

"Earth, air, fire, water. So that's three, and if you cube four it gives you sixty-four."

"Gee," says Colorado, "you've got it all worked out."

Kentucky says, "Well—not all."

I digest the shell and the egg with my lunch, and afterwards the three of us walk back to the villa; we finish packing, and tote our luggage—Texas has at last recovered his—inland to the lecture hall.

Here a few hundred students are standing in the sun upon the steps or along the street or in the foot-pocked sand between the villas, with suitcases and shopping bags around their feet. The buses to carry us to Punta Umbria are now on hand, four blocks away. But they are still packed with the hundreds of students brought in from Punta Umbria an hour before; with their housing in La Antilla unassigned, no one knows how to get them out of the buses and us in. So for the next hour we continue to stand, and they continue to sit.

Texas says, twice, "Why don't we get a cab?"

I say, the second time, "You don't need no course in the science of creative intelligence," and off we go in search of a phone.

The proprietor of a bar in one of the high-rises makes a call to Lepe for us, and thirty minutes later the two of us are back in a small cab to pick up Colorado and our bags. At the last minute my son, in conflict between conformity and comfort, succumbs and says he'll come with us; so we load his luggage and ours into the cab, and then cannot get in ourselves. Five other students now ask to be squeezed in with us. The driver and I have a gesticulative conversation, with my half in Spanish and his in I think Sanskrit, after which he drives away with the luggage. Texas not without alarm watches his disappear again—I reassure him that the driver has said he'll take our bags and return with a larger car, but he may also have said he'll sell our bags and move to a larger city. An hour later the uncertainty ends, he drives back in the same car with a rack clamped on the roof.

We repack our luggage on it, get in, promise the

five we'll send the cab back for them, and ride off waving goodbye to all. The cab is to cost each of us a buck and a half, and the other students follow us in the buses three hours afterwards.

23

And so goodbye to La Antilla, which I am not likely to see again, if indeed I ever saw it; intent on cosmic consciousness, we lived at the tide's edge like a colony of clams.

In the realtor's office there hung a big aerial photo of the town in summertime, its beach dotted with thousands of sunbathers, a vista of mass joy which made me shudder; but these lives were not unknown to me. On the weekends which bracketed our silence the sun brought a half-dozen families down in cars to their villas, middle-class Spaniards from the cities. In respectable garb, they sat on their porch furniture taking the sun, the high-heeled mothers yelled at the children, and the husbands escaped with their surfing-rods a mile up the beach, where like their counterparts on Cape Cod they stood all day casting in vain. Multiply these week-enders by a thousand and add a hot sun, I had been in that photo plenty of times.

It was its winter negative that charmed me, when other life was visible.

Dawns along the lonely beach would get me out to run, and on the gleaming flats I would jump at intervals the stakes and the narrow nets which disappeared into the ripples of low tide; sometimes there would be a swarthy fisherman in an old sweater, old pants tucked into rubber boots, standing out in the sea calf-deep to check the catch. Our dialogue was always the same:

"Are fish?"

"Yes, but are none."

They never spoke first. They were from a settlement a half-mile west of the villas, a low plastered tenement and shacks back in the dry sands, busy with women and children and dogs, and on their shelly beach stood a few longboats, full of oars. I never saw them launched, but at evening when one came in everybody running would haul and push to get it up above high water—the women tugging at its bow rope over their shoulders, the men thrusting at its stern and thwarts, the boys scurrying from back to front with logs underneath, its moveable roadbed.

These women were like rocks, their sexuality not for the eye, and in the mornings at low tide I often saw them strung out in a vigorous pantomime for hours along the wavelets. Barefoot, each had in one hand a stick on which to lean, and in the other a net bag on a handle, and they moved backwards in a sinuous dance of pelvis and working heels; they were ploughing in the soaked sand, and netting the clams their feet turned up. Vacationers and students could come and go, but this clam dance had been passing from mothers to daughters for centuries.

They and their men worked the sea like a farm, a poor one. All night it winked with a scatter of lights; I would see the boats in the day, a third of a mile out, with six or eight men oaring. I suppose they were laying other nets, because once I came upon a score of these men and women in a tug-of-war with the sea, straining to walk out of it a rope as thick as my wrist and so interminable I couldn't stay for its secret. Old and young, each woman and man on the rope wore a shoulder harness of cordage, with a tail ending in a wooden block; the one furthest inland would leave the line and descend past the others to the water and flog the rope with this tail, its block wrapping itself twice around, and so connected, slim rope to thick rope, would turn and drive against his harness—crying like a gull, "Olé olé olé olé!"—until he was again the one furthest inland; slacking his effort would disconnect him from the organism. It was like the beaching of the longboat, a secular ritual in which each knew his place, was both integer and sum; they were living what we were seeking.

And losing it. The sand that buried the streets was cleared by two horses with a plank drag, but hardly a day went without a youth on a motorcycle humming along the beach like a highway; three blocks inland the modern apartments were going up under the long necks of cranes—still with a folk touch, the "two-by-four" studs between floor and floor were the twisty trunks of young eucalyptus trees; television aerials were sprouting on rooftops, drawing down the images of far cities which would beckon the children away from the brutal hauling of nets and teach them the finer things and send their children back as vacationers, women in lipstick and men with surfing-rods.

Or perhaps as meditators. It did not suffice, the ritual of the nets, and so every evening at mass in the little iglesia the padre would offer the eucharist. It too for centuries had been, the bread of life; the riddle of eternity around me and my son at the sea's edge was around these fishermen, but now there were fewer takers. The loaf was mouldy, and my son was after strange gods.

At every other sunrise a tinkling would drift up the cold beach and soon a mirage would plod into view at my verandah, a hundred goats with udders hanging almost to the sand, tended by a few ragged men and boys with dogs, materializing from somewhere in the west and dumbly filing by and evaporating somewhere in the east, except for the road of their hoofmarks in the sand; at sunset their tinkling would drift back, and the mirage would pass again and be gone. On the last day of silence I hiked east for miles, and with the town lost behind me I went into a secret land of dunes, and was halted at last by the current of a wide river spreading into the sea; across it was a village of docks and boats, and miles further on the high-rises of Punta Umbria stood out of the sea, but on this side of the river I saw no herbage for that plodding procession of goats. Where they came from, and what green pasture they sought, I never learned, but I felt they had a lot in common with all of us.

24

Punta Umbria was ten or twelve miles off along the coast, but the way, with sand, marsh, and river, was impassable; the inland road was about thirty miles. It lay behind red clay cliffs, over a couple of bridges and through a swelling countryside of olive trees and orange trees, and out along a high ridge overlooking the sea from a forest of umbrella pine which I think lent the point its name. The serenity gave out abruptly, the land flattening, as we entered the boom town.

It was ten times the size of the one we had left, a year-round town, and began with a half-mile of buildings in construction; the scene was like what might greet the eye when emerging from the subway into a new development on the Brooklyn shore. Everywhere were bulldozers, generators, compressors. Between the beach and the avenue sat compounds of elegant two-story condominiums, four families per cube, separated by low redbrick walls; in from the avenue, where the land would bear the weight, towered a bulwark of new hotels and apartment-houses a dozen stories high. Most were unoccupied for the winter. Under them the avenue sported a few night clubs with signs in

English—The Jazz Bar, The American Bar—and then was lined for a mile with silent residences on its way into the business district. The avenue itself was trenched for new sewer lines, as was every side street, and the fat pipes lay helter-skelter atop endless mounds of sandy earth; the town looked like a battlefield.

One of these hotels, half of another, and a host of private apartments in the buildings between, were what MIU had taken over as a second campus. In the main hotel the lobby was stripped bare for us, rugless, scant of lounge furniture. Here a meditator presiding at the desk sent my housemates to a double upstairs; my son went off to a bed in a five-room apartment on a tenth floor two blocks away; and I took my suitcase to a double in the hotel, eighth floor front, where the door was opened by a lovely little blonde.

I said, presenting my door card, "I get you with the room?"

She said, returning it, "Would you like me to go down to the desk with you?"

I ended up in a single, with bath, second floor rear. It was an anywhere room—small bed, desk, chair, coffee-table, all cheaply modern—and had a balcony five feet square from which I could view the smokestacks of Huelva, lit all night and streaming all day. But there in a clump of greenery stood a finger of marble, a monument in the monastery which Columbus had made his headquarters; between me and it, unseen, lay the river out of which the three brief ships had sailed. Under the balcony was the delivery area of the hotel, with a collection of garbage drums, bounded by a sagging wire fence.

My room was off the corner of the stairwell, which led down into the center lobby, now converted into a dining-room for us. It was full of square tables with folding wooden chairs, and a long table offering the customary wealth of good foods; later the babble of voices and clatter of chairs bred rumors of a silent dining-room to be set up elsewhere, which remained rumors. In the back was a circular chamber with tall windows, the true dining-room, now converted into our meeting hall. Packed with a few hundred seats facing two TV sets on high stands, it was here that the course of videotapes began on the morning after our arrival.

On a figurative tether of three hundred feet from my bed to breakfast to my class to lunch to my class to my dinner to my class to my bed, I need never have taken my nose outside the glass doors; I was back in the hotel life I thought I had escaped.

25

It didn't matter much; I was on the spiritual rise, more benevolent each day, intrigued by the course and caught up in the fever of talk it begot at every table in the dining-room. Such talk was the other half of the course—the pedagogic concept itself had little room for it. In any case, since we were nine days late in starting, our schedule was crammed from ten in the morning till ten-thirty at night; in the next eighteen days we had one day off.

After meditation and breakfast we filed into the hall, about three hundred students. A dozen chairs in the second row—tactfully labelled "40+"—were reserved for us deaf and blind oldsters; from several countries, we included a city planner, a teacher, a surveyor, a private secretary, others. Three of us were men. The bulk of the gathering were college youth from America—both sexes, but no blacks, and when I asked why, one student thumbed his fingertips to signify money. Some pockets of European youth were marked by a mutter of translation throughout the proceedings. Our course leader was a slim fair-skinned young man who I was told had been Maharishi's driver for a year; himself we were to see only twice. But on every lap in the hall was a thick blue notebook with his pensive face on the cover, all bought in the co-op.

The young man introduced the first lecture by dictating a "summary of the main points"; we wrote them down verbatim. Thus primed, we watched the tape in color on the TV sets. With Guru Dev's portrait behind him, Maharishi sat cross-legged on a divan, flower in hand, and spoke without notes for half an hour; the camera work was restricted, mostly to his face in close-up, with a stealthy approach or retreat, and three reliable cuts, one to the flower, one to Guru Dev's portrait, one to a pan shot of an audience—the thirty-three lectures had been given live the winter before, on short notice, a rather remarkable performance. Listening, we were not to take notes, but many did. When the TV sets went blank, the young man read out to us a "long summary" of what we had heard; we wrote it down in paraphrase, our third time through it. The young man now introduced the second lecture by dictating a "summary of the main points", which we wrote down verbatim. Thus primed, we watched the tape in color on the TV sets; with Guru Dev's portrait behind him, Maharishi sat cross-legged on a divan, flower in hand— And so on, the procedure was unvarying. The two lectures, with the dictation, filled the morning.

After lunch, we convened again and broke up into small groups of a dozen or so, meeting in the hall and odd corners of the hotel; each had a leader named from its ranks. Ours was a cool boy, Jesuitschooled, who had already taken the course in Italy and taught it in Austria. It was his duty to grade us, and he explained the three grades: the lowest was "improving", which you received if you came in falling down drunk and had to be carried out, the next was "good", given when you weren't carried out, and the third was "excellent", average for the course.

I had some interesting questions on the lectures—interesting to me, I mean—but the pedagogy offered no time for them. The leader had a few mimeographed pages of others, a dozen on each tape, which he dictated to us; we took them down verbatim. A silent period ensued, while we wrote out the two dozen answers in brief, consulting our earlier notes for the wording in the lecture. Done, we were each then assigned one of the questions to answer at length, two when they outnumbered us, and another period of silent writing ensued; most in my group wrote small essays. Finally, each student got to his feet in turn—for practice in public speaking—and read his essay answer out to us; with some latitude, its correctness was judged by its fidelity to Maharishi's words, quoted on the leader's mimeographed page. One query per essay was allowed from the group, to which the standee's answer was improvised—it was the cadenza minute in a rigid form, dedicated to the purity of the teaching.

This meeting filled the afternoon. We broke then, to write letters, wash out our socks, shop in a nearby supermercado, meditate, and eat dinner. Over it, Texas grumbled:

"It's strange no creative intelligence is welcome in a course on creative intelligence."

In the evening we massed again in the hall. The young man read to us a "short summary" of the first tape, after which we watched it once more; now we had an interval of half an hour or so for questions, the young man's responses, and further opinions from the floor; he then read to us a "short summary" of the second tape, and we watched it again. In various forms, we had now been through each of the two lectures six times in the course of the day, and were familiar with it. The evening ended with the three hundred of us rising for a puja in Sanskrit, sotto voce—I was the most sotto, the only student not in training as an initiator, and ignorant of the text; but I knelt at the appropriate moment with the others, like a good Catholic.

It was over lunch and dinner, and in the rooms at night, that the real talk came; at every meal I set my tray down to a different knot of heads to drink it in. Colorado had shown me the back of an envelope on which his mother had penned her final thought for the world to read, "The Brain in Spain Is Going Down the Drain"—nothing was less true. Not since my own youth in "the" movement had I been in such a hotbed of intellectual ferment. Skeptical or devout, yet all believers, these young folk were bright, many of them trained in the physical sciences, and highly logical; they shared a conviction that meditation had brought them to the brink of a new revelation, and were inquiring into its structure. So all the topics of man's quest—epistemology, fate, the root of evil, free will, matter and mind, the afterlife—were their small talk, between bites. I was the freak among them; Colorado introduced me with a jerk of the thumb, "*He* doesn't believe in reincarnation!"

Too late for quoting I heard that Maharishi, fondling a flower, had said, "One carnation is enough."

It was the extremists who most fascinated me. In their dialectic on the common premise they erected by immaculate interconnections of logic a superstructure like a castle in the air with a countless number of rooms, wherein I felt I could wander forever, and not come down to earth. I even considered, keeping in mind the egg and the shell, it might be true.

The premise was that the world in which I had lived all my life was but half the story—life is a dream, who has not thought so?—and the reality that underlay it was "the absolute", the home of truth, wisdom, love. So much was the property of every religion, but it was no act of faith, to them; many had been there, on drug trips, and fallen out of it, and were hungry to live in it permanently, like Maharishi. Me too. But to reject the phenomenal world meant throwing out—and this was the price-tag I wasn't about to pay—seven centuries of rational procedures the western hemisphere had painfully accumulated to comprehend it.

"I've been told on *very* high authority that he"—said a boy from the floor of our meeting, after naming the bald old pundit—"knows how to get to the moon, and could have told NASA beforehand."

On perhaps the same authority, it was proposed to another meeting that such jumps in evolution as were seen in mutations could be effected by meditation. This view, expressed by a visiting speaker, was questioned from behind me by a young male voice, a bit troubled:

"Gee, I don't think we ought to make that statement, it implies meditation can change the gene structure."

"Oh, I'm sure it must," said the speaker, "or how could we remember our past lives?"

I didn't see how, but some fundamentalists believed in an angelic order the way I believed in the hotel's upper floors. Over lunch the surveyor, yes, the surveyor laid out for me the sixteen strata of consciousness in the cosmos, ranging from zero through mineral, vegetable and animal to man, who occupied three, and thence on to angels, archangels, deities—all to be visible when we were sufficiently enlightened. I said that would be nice, and a boy who was listening said calmly:

"Of course, we have people here who have been on those levels, and come back."

I said, curious, "Who?"

"Maharishi, for one."

For him and others, Maharishi thus was infallible,

literally. Perhaps this tenet was an elaboration of his saying that in the highest state of consciousness "all decisions are spontaneously right", which made human sense, but much of what he said I thought was corrupted by such students into a literalism which didn't. It was doubt-proof—I heard repeatedly that Maharishi's words, from his level, could be cognized only fragmentarily on ours—and it dissolved even the corruption itself. In my small group, restless with its gossip of the naked eye's ability to see electrons in the sixth state, I quoted Maharishi that we "do better to go to western science" for knowledge of such matters, and I added:

"When I listen to Maharishi himself, he sounds a lot more sane and sound and sensible than when you guys talk about him."

There was a moment's silence.

"Of course he does," one then said, grinning, "he's in a higher state of consciousness!"

I joined in the laugh; but there was a grain of something cruel in the adoration, the leader co-operating as victim, infallibility is a thorny crown. Late one night at the elevator a handful of us gathered around a hypnotic anecdote—told by the slim blond seminarian of the Christmas mass—of Maharishi's love for sugar cubes: whenever he visited a certain hostess in California she put a plateful in front of him to nibble until, replete, he begged her to take them away. One boy stood with a grave face, and then asked:

"Did you see that yourself?"

"No," said the seminarian, "I heard it from the hostess."

"Well. If I were you," the boy said coldly, "I wouldn't spread a story like *that* unless I'd seen it myself."

This was the boy who thought Maharishi had come back from the angels. The love of such believers allowed the master no leeway as a man; descending the platform after a visit to us at Punta Umbria, he stumbled on a step—a gasp froze the crowd, and afterwards there was a buzz in certain clumps of the literalists, how could he stumble? was it true that in Boston at a dark stairway backstage he'd asked why there was no light?—the incident was incomprehensible. It was at odds with the fact that the deer skin on his divan, which later I learned he sat on for cleanliness, was to "ground" his emanations, otherwise hazardous to us.

In the midst of such neo-medievalisms I was relieved to see on the bulletin board in the lobby, under a scribble that Foreman had TKO'd Joe Frazier in the second, another scribble:

"What's your source?"

My social life was thus never boring, full of surprises, and quickened by the perplexity of the cosmic. Although I wrote my wife that "by any old-fashioned standard everyone here is mad", it was only when the wind was north-north-west; these schizophrenics were totally sane. I thought the wild talk was itself a good part of the current of unification, individual and communal, which made for sanity. Even with my eyebrows up, I felt lucky to listen; all my sons, the encampment was on a cliff at land's end, overlooking an ocean unknown to man.

And these divers into it always climbed back on land. When one of Maharishi's tapes violated their sense of logic, it provoked a two-day rebellion, war in heaven; but that's a later chapter.

26

The first hour after waking, and a second before dinner, and the last in bed before I turn my light off, are the three I have to myself in the day's routine; they are too scattered—and the rumors of that unknown ocean too lively—for me to get on with the writing that filled the evenings of silence week.

As for the relative ocean, in the hotel there is no sense whatever of its life three blocks away; but I still get out to it between meditation and breakfast, picking my way at dawn through the excavated streets to run on the beach. It's less fun, no longer spontaneous, and much less lovely under a thousand windows, but good enough until a couple of other things put an end to it. The first is a persistent ache in a toe of my right foot; it seems I have broken it.

Or so I am advised by the young seminarian, who once suffered the same mishap running barefoot; in the seminary he was a track man. Friends now, we enjoy a number of heady powwows on religion and meditation, usually at midnight in my room over a bottle of red wine and sardines, smuggled in. The wine is half sinful in this community, as is too much exercise; and he recalls a meet in which he was the favorite, running the 880 in two laps, so embarrassed to be last in a field of fifteen that he sprinted the entire second lap—"which nobody does"—and came in first. It "wrecked" his lungs, for days he couldn't breathe without coughing.

"Everyone here would call it a terrible stress," he says, "but I lived for a month on that win, it's one of the memorable experiences of my life."

"Oh, Kevin," says his other friend, a Canadian girl, "it'll be a pity when the rest of us are in cosmic consciousness and you're just 880 yards short."

Despite this hazard I continue to run mornings, but in my sneakers; favoring my right foot, I next pull a tendon behind my left ankle, which fattens to twice its size, and for a week I can barely hobble upstairs. During the week I catch the head cold which everyone is passing on from spoon to spoon, hundreds of meditators blowing into hankies, and for the rest of the course my running is confined to my nose. Older and wiser, I keep my broken toe and bulging ankle half a secret from my son, who I think is devoted to the superior wisdom of Maharishi enough already.

I could however take my feet and nose to the doctor; we have three in attendance round the clock. I am acquainted with one who let my wife have an antibiotic for a sore throat, and with the others by two bits of hearsay.

One bit is from Colorado, who is glum. During silence he was rounding twelve hours a day and moved into my villa saying, "Boy, do I feel sassy!" —then broke it off abruptly for our move; now he is moody, has a bedtime brandy or two alone at The Jazz Bar, makes objections from the floor to all the tapes, is "unstressing". He's across the hall from me, and when I look in to inquire after his soul he says it's "not good", he's going to the clinic. The doctor prescribes a foot massage. It's administered in his room, which also puzzles me, until I find him prostrate on the bed after it; the masseur has worked on nothing but his feet for an hour and a half, and Colorado shows me the towel he's been biting on to keep from screaming. It seems to work, like shock therapy, he is cheerier.

The massages are celebrated, and I am almost tempted, until the seminarian requests one for a backache and is given acupuncture instead. I ask did the needles bother him.

"No," he says, "what bothered me was the doctor while putting them in kept looking it up in a handbook."

So I count on nature, and now spend the hour before breakfast in bed with an anthology on prayer, lent to me by the seminarian; I dip into it again before I turn my light off for the night. It's the same ocean, the unknown, and what interests me is to bring together the intimations of it which eluded me in my Catholic infancy and the rumors of it which baffle me in my Hindu dotage. Meanwhile, on the night shelf at my elbow lies the notebook with the dozen pages I have written, merely secular.

27

They are part of a monograph I began prior to our trip, born of a seminar in playwriting I had taught at a university for a couple of years; its subject is the structure of dramatic tension in Shakespeare. In a word, form. I am thinking about it now in a new context, the distaste for "stress" in this community, whose aim is to purify it out of everyone's nervous system; it is a pollutant. It seems to me playwrights are thus in a peculiar business, the deliberate manufacture of it.

In my experience, whenever I neglected to build enough stress into a play I had a flop. I learned also that success is no good and failure is worse—an old wisdom, the work must be done for itself, which in this system is the counsel to "act, but detach from the fruits of action". That is, act without a feedback of conflict over the outcome. But of all the arts the theatre is the most public, it does not exist without an audience, and the will to success is ingrained in its practice. The wooing of the audience is half of the art, and it lies in building a tension of stresses that no one wants to walk away from.

The "form" in which this is essayed is as old as the Bhagavad Gita, and not without a wisdom too.

In twenty-five centuries it has undergone so many changes of time and place and fashion that to generalize is clearly foolish; and since by form I mean "everything in the piece" each work itself presents its own, a specific variant of the current fashion. But I don't mind being clearly foolish, I believe the drama as a form mirrors a constant in the human mind, and I'll use the structural wont of its greatest practitioner as a kind of classic norm. It cannot be irrelevant; and it has its equivalences in all dramatic literature, up to our day.

This five-minute tour of the centuries will be in three long breaths, the exposition, the working-out, and the denouement.

When does a play begin?—in the moment when a state of equilibrium is disrupted by a new happening, and not before. Imagine a court in which the old king has died, his brother has succeeded to the throne and married the widow, and her young son is in mourning; the aging newlyweds are happy, and all is stable. I say imagine because we do not see it, the playwright has no time for such a tableau, stability is not his first business. Instead, into our sight walks at once a ghost, that of the dead king, and we learn that it "bodes some strange eruption to our state"; this is the happening, and its function is not only to bode, but to bring about. It unbinds the energies implicit in the equilibrium, which is thrown into imbalance, and will not be restored until the playwright has taken us through five acts of stress and counter-stress.

How?—by each character's move. The appearance of the ghost is a pawn opening; those who witness it must move next. But a move seeks an object,
the object here is the son, and their move will be
to tell him the spirit of his father is haunting the
premises. It's a promise they make us on the spot;
our interest is not in will they keep it—they must,
an unkept promise is like cheating at chess, we aban-
don the game—but in "what will happen", that is,
what further imbalance their move will force.

This encounter of move and object, called a
scene, implies that in it one or the other will be altered: the move initiates a scene, the alteration ends
it—the alteration is the new imbalance. In the monograph on my night shelf it takes me ten pages to
say that, with evidence; here I wish only to emphasize that the scene is a fundamental human invention, like the wheel, and the history of western
theatre rides on it.

The business of the scene at hand is to unleash the
protagonist of the play. Given the news, the son is
quickened out of his melancholia, or altered from
object into move; he will seek the ghost himself.
The ghost is now the object, and the scene between
them is the promise. Note, each promise grows more
potent in turn. Keeping this one, the son learns the
equilibrium is a sham—the ghost tells all, the mother
was adulterous with his brother, he himself was
poisoned, and the son is to revenge him. In this cli-
mactic scene of the exposition, it is the move now
that is altered. The ghost fades out, much the same;

but the son's action has been fed and swells into the resolve "to set it right", the master move of the play. It is a promise, tension, stress, which four centuries of playgoers have found it impossible to walk out on.

This thumbnail image of the act suggests little of its true substance; it is among the greatest of expositions, catches up in its progress every force latent in the past and every character to be used in the future—I am speaking only of its action, I dare not even mention the language—and ends in a revelation of the two antagonists. But I am concerned here with form, not with the substance it cannot be separated from. The crux of every exposition, whose task is to open the past and future to our eye, lies in the discovery of the antagonists. Step by step, the technical devices peculiar to drama—the happening, the move, the scene—take us deeper into its nature. The first move, telling the son, breaks the surface; the second, seeking the ghost, is a journey to know the underworld of the past; the third, promising revenge, is a vow to confront the enemy. It is a descent into the psychic realm of conflict.

The working out of this conflict, by a linkage of widening moves and scenes, constitutes the body of a play. Each move by a character is a decision, an act of will, seeking its object; each object is a character, capable of decision, quickened to an act of will. Thus, in the body of a play, the scene is a unit not only of move against object, but of will against will.

So, in this play, the suspect king and the reveng-ing son commence their circling of each other; they must come to grips. What keeps them apart?—neither is certain of what is in the other's mind. This is the overt barrier, and their separate schemes to probe it make for the famous scenes of the next two acts. The king looses spies upon the son, two friends from college and a girl he has loved; it doesn't work, the son berates her and mocks them. The son con-spires with actors to present a play—a play! the form we are investigating is his instrument of investiga-tion—which parallels the ghost's tale; it does work, the king flees the hall in panic. And at his prayers, alone, he confesses his deed. Now at last, three acts into the question, we know the answer; nothing re-mains but for the son to stab the king. But he can-not.

Why?—because he is not after the king, he is after his mother. The worse crime is her adultery, it obsesses him not only in his beratings of the girl but throughout the mock play itself; and when im-mediately after it he "cleaves her heart in twain"—a scene of spiritual rape—it's for her lust, he forgets to inquire whether she had a hand in his father's murder. The covert barrier between him and the king is in himself. It lurks in his every flailing solilo-quy on his "cowardice"; the outward conflict be-tween good and evil is erected on an inward conflict in the individual. It is at that conflictual depth that the play is obscure, modern, imperfect, compelling.

Its denouement is thus the outcome of two levels

of conflict; the king moves on one, the son on both. The king's move after his exposure is to ship the son off to be killed in a foreign land; he escapes and comes back. But not to move in turn, even to revenge himself, the violent scene with his mother has left him strangely depleted, almost fulfilled. And it is not until the moment she dies by mistake on the king's poison that the son keeps his promise—revenges *her*, stabs the king, and into his dying mouth pours the same cup. Death engulfs the three; when a new ruler enters, all the forces of the conflict have played themselves out, nothing unused, nothing left over, stasis. The denouement is accomplished, it has restored a state of equilibrium.

Which is the equilibrium of the state, as in most of this author's plays; such content is what changes with time and place, not the dynamic of conflict.

It's a thoroughly unpleasant tale, replete with the stresses we avoid in life, why do we pay money for it? Because it is "art", and the stresses are mastered by a means practiced for more than two millennia to agitate and lift our souls, and leave them in a fuller tranquility. The linkage of moves and scenes is more than a technique for telling a story; it is the bonework of drama, will against will. The form itself is thus an image of the divisions in the mind of every spectator. That the son as playwright uses it to discover truth almost mocks our own attendance; we are "guilty creatures sitting at a play" to learn a truth in ourselves. The play is a vicarious conflict we pay to have. As in life itself, each colliding of will against will ends in a temporary victory of one, forcing the other into a wider field of battle, their energies filling their space, until they are exhausted in a transcendent reconciliation which includes all, as in death itself. There is no victor but Allah. The play is a vicarious conflict we pay to have resolved. The celebrated catharsis of which we read is experienced only in that resolution, and it happens in comedy too; and what makes all this stress a "play" and worth the money is that a resolution in the end is assured from the beginning.

But who are these characters in a hubbub, talking, poisoning, coming back from the dead, kissing, weeping, putting on plays, stabbing, going mad, making jokes, jumping into graves, duelling and dying, and coming to final terms: and where do they really live? They are voices in the playwright's head.

Which brings us to the doorknob of cosmic consciousness.

28

In my own head the old boy's language too was floating around; when in our small group I made a point about imagery the quote on my tongue—and hardly by chance—was, "Bare ruin'd choirs, where late the sweet birds sang." Midway in the course, we visited one.

Well, it wasn't really ruin'd, although it had seen a lot of wear over the centuries, including a historic earthquake. It was in use still as a Franciscan monastery. The finger of marble visible from my window stood in its gardens on the edge of Huelva, and I had driven there the day I picked up the money at the bank; on our day off I went back in a boat with my son and five other students.

It was a small open boat, with an engine in its floor, which the young seminarian and I had rented the day before. Punta Umbria had been a fishing village first, and along its riverfront the old wooden houses with porches and the big nets spread out in the sun for mending and the wharf with gaudy boats riding at anchor had a color of detail missing from the boom end of town; in a large shed, around baskets crammed with fish and squid, men in sweaters listened to an auctioneer chanting in precisely the breakneck lingo of a tobacco auction in Virginia. The seminarian and I had come to look for a ferry—the usual route to the monastery, two miles off as the gull flew, was a dozen miles inland by bus—but there was none. Soon we had a committee gathered around us, who went off in different directions and brought back a fisherman willing to take us next day for thirteen dollars, and we clinched the deal in a bar over a glass of good malaga for seven cents, which they insisted on treating us to. We chatted about the boom and life in the town; before, everybody knew everybody else, now everybody was making more money.

"And is more content?" I asked.

"No," one of them said with a wry smile, "more money and more content are things different."

Why, then?—it was the question our students were asking; the world had tilted, and willy-nilly we were all sliding off it into a money pit.

Next morning the seven of us marched to the wharf and were met by our shy fisherman, and followed him down across a bigger vessel as a stepping-stone into his boat; scattered on the bow and the thwarts, with him at the tiller, we putputted out and upriver. It was deltoid here, with long marshy islands in it, below the confluence of two rivers at the monastery. To get there we had to pass under the Huelva smokestacks, from which a solid bank of grey smog poured seaward; entering it, we coughed and wept tears for ten minutes, but emerged to chug past a powerful concrete giant—Columbus—who over a cross stood gazing west, and at last drew to the bank opposite and a dock. With the fisherman, we climbed a narrow back road between trees to the cloisters on the hill. At the weathered doors we waited till the half-hour, when it was permitted to sound the pullbell—it was, after all, a monastery at prayers—and soon an elderly monk in a brown robe opened a panel and let us in.

We stepped out of our time. The half of the monastery lived in by the monks was not to be seen, but part of their work was to keep the ancient half as a museum; and here in room after room were relics of the era when Spain sailed into its greatness. Swords, maps, crucifixes, paintings hung on the walls, and in three glass cases bristled the four-foot replicas of the Pinta and Santa Maria and Nina, audacious wee beauties, and in this bedchamber Columbus had lived, outfitting them in the river below for a voyage over the cataract at the edge of the world. But it was not these I had come back to, it was the otherworld of the monastery itself.

It too had been meditating, for centuries, and we followed the old monk through it in a kind of envy. It was not of extraordinary beauty, although one room—the refectory in its heart, with a pulpit in the wall overlooking its heavy wood tables, where the monks had given thanks for their daily bread five centuries ago—was a work of art. The inner patio, surrounded by a walk of old bricks between the wall frescos of moorish arabesque and the colon-naded arches, let in the light of heaven on growing things; and from other arches on an outer balcony upstairs we looked out over orchard and garden descending to the river. In these haunts the ghosts of robed monks walking with their prayerbooks were almost as believable as our guide. He was a brown dumpling of an old saint with cropped white hair, who had served a lifetime of poverty, chastity, and obedience among the Indians of South America, and was toddling to his grave, but with a pixie's humor; he did jerky imitations of Indians shooting arrows at Columbus, and mumbled jokes, and the clarity in his face was a wonder to us. It was a translucence my son and these students were after, and its source we saw when he took us into the shadowy chapel. Here in the altar light hung the crucified son of man, half life-size, sagging with starved ribs and twisted head, mouth open in death, a marvellous and harrowing piece; it was said in the movement that Jesus was so evolved he had felt nothing—a notion I detested, it cut the heart out of the paradox—but this fourteenth-century sculptor knew better. At the candle-rack one of our two girls dropped coins into the box and lit seven candles, one for each of us.

After an hour we left, reluctant, and stood in the sunlight of our own time, getting used to our expulsion. One boy said:

"I'm ready to move in."

But instead we ate a hearty meal for two hours in an hosteria on the grounds, and met up with four more meditators, acquiring two as passengers, and went with our fisherman down again to the dock. Heading home in the river's flow we passed once more under the concrete giant, the other statue, a man of action who had sailed out on this water and crossed three thousand miles of sea and come upon a continent of incalculable wealth which, after five teeming centuries in the getting of worldly power, had given birth to us—and we were back to his starting point, looking for the peace he had sailed away from. I mean, talk about your ferry rides to nowhere—

At the wharf I paid the fisherman, who refused the three-dollar tip I offered, so we shook hands instead, and the nine of us walked back to the hotel and into our spectrum of videotapes.

29

On the other hand, sex.

This will be a short chapter, with no autobiographical content at all, alas. My wife's talk was still reverberating in some heads, and in my small group a boy buttressed an opinion of his own by quoting her:

"As that lady said—"

I said, "That was no lady, that was my wife."

The word got around, and in the forty-plus row a gracious woman next to me said impulsively:

"That was your wife? Give her my love."

Such reflected glory was pleasant, but it did make fidelity somewhat compulsory. Actually, an observer of the community would have thought sexual life part of the unmanifest; the young females made no effort to be sexy, by finery or gewgaws, and the young males maintained what might be called a low profile. Minimally, the female look could be ascribed to living for months out of a suitcase. Only one handsome couple dressed with such sexual awareness of themselves that I finally asked were they in show biz—kind of, commercial art—and when I then asked how many suitcases, they lamented a sizeable one lost forever down the native tongue.

Maximally, the look was part of the ideological climate which, as in other revolutions, was rather puritanical.

Sex as salvation—the niche it fills in any world dead to other hopes—was a hurdle on the true ascent. Maharishi's celibacy set a tone; it was honored, even in the breach. I was not surprised to be told that each local center was in receipt of a directive which requested no hanky-panky under the roof, though I thought it went too far when I heard we had a newlywed couple who were celibate. Still, the flesh is the flesh.

The monogamous was visible, even audible. In our course were two marriages complete with toddlers, who played in an adjoining room until they emitted bleats of despair, when our young leader sighed happily, "Sounds of bliss," and the parents rushed to save them. And we had a few other couples, some married, some not, who descended to breakfast hand in hand. Less visibly, the seminarian —who wasn't entering the priesthood because there were "so many other things to do", and I guessed what—had a bedtime problem; his roommate was often busy with a guest under the blankets. In another course the Canadian girl had roomed with a seventeen-year-old, just discovering men, who welcomed so many of them into bed that the Canadian put a hand over her eyes and told herself "this isn't happening".

So the range was normal enough, considering that the flesh was not why we were here. As for the

celibate newlyweds, hearsay was that neither en-
joyed the sexual relation, they had different tastes
anyway, and didn't like doing things together; celibacy was all they had in common.

I include these physiological studies so as to be
scientifically exhaustive, and literarily up-to-the-
minute. The topic is not without significance; I just
don't know any more. In extension of it the seminarian asked another question:

"This course is a survey of life, where is the idea
of growth through human relatedness?"

30

The ideology of the movement is a sampling of that body of Vedantic philosophy, "an atheistic religion", which took form so early in man's history it may antedate the invention of writing, and has been accumulating since by commentary and revision—including Maharishi's—for three thousand years; it is one of the great systems of human thought, and for me to give a summary of it in ten minutes is ridiculous. Nevertheless, I will do it.

We begin with the absolute and the relative. The relative is what we are accustomed to think of as "the real world"; it is characterized by objects, the boundaries of time and place, diversity, the conflict of opposites, incessant flow and change, mortality. And, imperfect knowledge of it. In this everyday world we live and work, and although "life evolves to be lived in abundance"—I'll be quoting Maharishi throughout—and the "enjoyment of more and more" to the end of fulfilment, when we look around us human experience "doesn't seem to be so". Why?—because we are starved for the absolute, which underlies all.

Everything that the relative is not, the absolute is; we define it as boundless, timeless and spaceless, omnipresent, changeless and eternal, one. It's close to what westerners think of as the Creator—not the personal figure, but that spirit of which one apostle wrote that "no man hath seen God at any time". The atheism is in part a matter of pronouns; the absolute is not Him, but It, a locution pleasant to liberated women, but otherwise lacking a certain warmth of concern. The relative world is its manifestation. From electron to galaxy, including man, all creation is the "play and display" of its energy; and this energy is what Maharishi calls "creative intelligence".

Or not quite. In speaking of the timeless, chronology is irrelevant; but we take the liberty of saying that, in the beginning, pure Intelligence is. "Is" implies existence. When Intelligence "prepares to play a role in its own field"—a phrase we will come back to—existence becomes "conscious", and Intelligence then becomes creative intelligence. "And God said, let there be light; and there was light." It becomes, that is, the force which manifests itself in electron, man, galaxy. Why does it need to?—unanswerable. It may be only as "play". The western answer is that the creature should praise its maker—applause, following the "play"—which may distinguish a culture interested in "the fruits of action" from one which is not.

The nature of this creative intelligence is "integrative", it unites the opposites of the cosmos—unmanifest and manifest, silence and activity. It creates not only all phenomena, but the changes in them; it is essentially evolutionary. In this work or play it is "progressive". It is "purposeful", towards an end which, like its beginning, I am not prepared to swear to; it is "discriminative, selectively precise, innovative, infallible" in its choice of moves; it is "self-sufficient", it creates everything "from within itself". It is "orderly" and "systematic", and its system is the invariable alternation of rest and activity. In small, we practice this alternation in the phases of meditation and daily action; and in large, what the west calls "eternity" is but an active phase of the cosmos, which returns to silence, to give birth to new eternities—a staggering view, but beautiful in the esthetic span and unity of the vision.

In this cosmology, the human nervous system is uniquely placed, midway. Inherent in it is the capability of "experiencing the full range" of creative intelligence—from the "grossest" manifestation of an object, through the "subtlest" values of its subatomic structure, to "pure consciousness" without content. When I asked a visiting leader why this uniqueness of our nervous system, he said it was "like asking why red is red"; but it parallels having been made in God's image. In both cases, of course, it is man talking about man. Our uniqueness in this system means that in theory we have waking access to that reservoir of creative intelligence which is the absolute. It is blocked in practice by the accumulation in us of stresses, psychic and physiological; hence the passion for purification. And Dr. Bronner's soap.

But at what point, in a cosmos which is infallibly progressive, arises the first "stress"? I can't say, ten minutes have exhausted my expertise; you must picture the three hundred of us in a buzz of table talk, all novices, tangled in the fascinating enigmas of the theory and with no authority to bring them to except a videotape. My own answer—that the relative is dualistic, and stress is the struggle of its opposites—was not acceptable to monists who understood Maharishi as saying "life is not a struggle"; and after a day's debate a group reported to our meeting their conclusion that "stress" is a perversity born of man's free will to choose. Which is also, of course, the origin of "sin".

Transcendental Meditation, together with the "right action" it leads us to, "refines" the nervous system as a channel to the absolute. All "suffering is based on weakness", certainly a truth, and the weakness meant is that of the mind, when deficient in creative intelligence; if the nervous system is purified of stress, and the mind flooded with the absolute, suffering is eliminated. So, in paintings of Saint Sabastian transfixed with arrows he is indifferent, his gaze on heaven.

The heart of the doctrine thus is the individual, the knower himself, and his state of consciousness. "Knowledge is structured in consciousness," a sentence from the Vedas, is MIU's motto; it means the quality of consciousness conditions the quality of its perceptions. To "know thyself" truly is to know the self as identical with the universal consciousness.

And it is by "transcending" the mantra in meditation—that is, dropping the mantra and all other mental content, while remaining conscious—that we cross into the universal.

This use of a mantra or something much like it is not unknown to western mystics; one in the fourteenth century counsels us to dwell upon a monosyllable, say "God" or "sin", that we may put a "forgetting" between us and the things of the world, even God's things, and so enter into a "cloud of unknowing" where, and only where, we contact him directly. And another counsels us to pray with a suspension of breath on each word of the prayer, a method comparable to alternate-nostril pranayama in its reduction of oxygen intake, with psychic after-effects.

In our group, this dipping into the void was not unambiguous. When it was first my turn in the small group to answer a question, I quoted the "correct" words about transcending in meditation; my questioner then muttered something I didn't catch. Later I asked him what it was, and he said again, "Do you have experiences like that?" I said no, and he said he didn't either, so I began asking around, and ran into a fog of no, maybe, not sure—it wasn't easy to distinguish from either a momentary blanking called "blackout" or just dozing off. Others were confident they transcended. For all, the fourth or transcendental state is the qualitative jump where the crucial act of faith in the theoretical system occurs; the higher states are predicated upon it.

With repeated dippings into the transcendental, we bring our awareness of it back into the "real" world after meditation; it fades there, of course. But it fades less each time, which is what "evolution" means, and eventually we own it for keeps. In the waking state, then, we perceive the boundaries of the relative with a consciousness retentive of the boundlessness of the absolute; we are in both states simultaneously, and therewith are said to be in the fifth, or "cosmic consciousness". Now the mind is "restful even in the midst of activity", a considerable gain. Conversely, it maintains its alertness even while sleeping—neither perceiving nor blanking out, but "resting in its own self-awareness"—and we sleep less.

Like a wide-angled lens which takes in a greater field, but vertically too, the fifth state now reveals "finer" values in the relative hidden from ordinary perception. With our consequently "more refined" choice of action "guided by the impulse of the heart", it penetrates to the subtlest level of objects— it's here that some students anticipate seeing electrons—and so becomes a sixth state. The sixth was formerly called "God consciousness", but at one meeting Maharishi said impatiently it "has nothing to do with God, it could as well be called ring-ding consciousness", and rechristened it as "glorified cosmic", or "g-c" for short.

But in every object, below its subtlest value, is the transcendental. It is identical with the transcendental in the knower. And now, moving through the finest veil of the relative, the knower joins the unboundedness in himself to the unboundedness in the object, "like to like"; subject and object become one. This is the seventh state, or "unity consciousness", and it is attended by the "bliss" of the boundless. In this state, where we have left behind us all the limitations of the individual ego, knowledge of the relative world is no longer imperfect. Our subjective means of knowledge, consciousness, has become as unchanging or "non-variable" as our objective means, science; more, it has opened to us the "infinite" value of every object. It is thus that we become "at home with everything", all our decisions are "spontaneously right", and we are "free from doubts about life".

Hogwash?

In western experience, these states are mirrored in the progress of mystical prayer "from Purgation through Illumination to Union"—with God, of course—the culmination of which was put into words by a writer in the fifteenth century: "The place where Thou art found unveiled is girt round with the coincidence of contradictories, and this is the wall of Paradise wherein Thou dost abide. 'Tis beyond the coincidence of contradictories that Thou mayest be seen and nowhere this side thereof."

Refinements beyond the seventh state were announced during the winter, and there are rumors of more, but the seventh as described indicates the nature of this "supreme knowledge" which beckons every meditator on. It's not a hope of heaven, but a certainty; what believer would jeopardize it by drugs, or other contaminations? And out of the ideological arise the organizational goals to regenerate the world.

MIU itself is to become a university with a full curriculum offering baccalaureate, master's, and doctoral degrees, on a schedule which alternates two months of academic study with one month of rounding; thus a doctorate would include more than two years of isolation in meditation, which some students take as a "guarantee" of unity consciousness. The movement is embarked upon a "world plan", with 3600 centers, whose objective is to deliver one teacher to every thousand persons on the planet. In that day, said my son's housemate, all job-applications will feature the question, "Are you a meditator?" Beyond the individual, the goals are social: to improve government, fulfil education, dissolve anti-social behavior, and lift man's environmental, economic, and spiritual life. In short, "end the chaotic history of the past" and man's suffering "in this generation". This achievement for mankind as a whole is more than possible, it is historically inevitable, "merely"—said one girl—"a matter of time".

It was a phrase much in our hearts in the thirties, and my memories of the psychic unification I experienced in that movement helped me to understand a good deal in this, but not all. The most striking difference here was "the technique" of periodic withdrawal from the world, and from one's "social" personality; during it one felt an inner quiet, a temporary deculturation, which aspired to a blanking out of the individual's own "chaotic history"; and on that tabula rasa, surfacing, the movement wrote its signature in terms much more familiar to me. It was, first, a family which broke in common the bread of total affirmation. It was united around a charismatic leader, second, and an ideology, third, which proved each other; the leader's infallibility derived from his exalted state of consciousness, and the attainment of that state was assured by an infallible leader. Thus, all were unburdened of the cares of individual will, and merged in the group will of —four—a great task, to convert and save the world. With its outcome inevitable, it was another kind of "play"; its resolution in the end was promised from the beginning.

A couple of my skunks were now in the pot—I knew why these youth were saved, and I saw a twinship between the Marxist hope and this one—but this was only social, or at least parlor, psychology; the one that wouldn't go in was number three, the exalted state itself, and it was the one which most interested and irritated me. Metaphysically, the likenesses in technique and doctrine between east and west were not remarkable. Man's intimations of divinity are based on his sense of what he is, and on his reach to what he is not; both, throughout the world, are something of a constant. But the witness to such states of mind from all times and lands is persuasive of their "reality"—not that our young, baptized in acid, need persuasion—and what vexed me was a pettier question, how come I'd been left out?

31

"I know Maharishi is as evolved as a man can be, but—"

Unstressing. It's my disgruntled son, mulling over the move as we walk one night from his apartment to my hotel, and it's the first but I've heard out of him. I'm both pleased and displeased; I don't enjoy his veneration of his master, but I know how significant it is in his growth.

Not to speak of mine. Nothing has taught me so much of myself as the ups and downs of fatherhood, and its most wistful down is the descent a father makes in his son's eye from omniscience to ignorance; but to love is to acquire another's eye, and the new worlds in it. Which is what the seminarian means by growth through human relatedness. I've begun to learn from my sons; and I think it's a little wicked that this boy, named by me after the apostle who wouldn't believe except he put his finger in the print of the nails, is not only himself a disciple of the unseen, but has sent me back to mass and monastery, hunting plums.

What he's disgruntled over is the ugliness of the new town and its noise, in the apartment below his a Spaniard is practicing piano through all his meditations. I see him less regularly here, we're in different programs, but he sometimes stops in at my room for a late chat or a shower. In his place the water is lukewarm, and in the other hotel it's cold; in ours it's hot, but for three days all the faucets are bone-dry, and the toilets throughout the new building must add up to a pretty sight for anyone in the seventh state. I don't think it's the pianist he's glum about, it's that the staff too is improvising again.

In my course, they're tripping over their feet in videotapes. Once, our tape starts in the middle of one lecture, minus the first half, and ends in the middle of another, minus the second half; next we run out of tapes altogether and wait for them to arrive by airmail from Los Angeles, but the meditator who travels up to Seville can't get them out of customs because they're labelled for someone else, and for two days we restudy tapes we've been through six times; when tape thirty-three is opened it turns out to be tape eighteen.

We guffaw over these mishaps, but I'm less amused by the improvisations in my son's program. It's something of a patchwork, and he feels he's "wasting time"; there will be no more rounding for anyone till my course is done, he is separated from Maharishi, they're making do piecemeal with odd tapes, and his sense of "really accomplishing something" is frazzling out. I'm troubled by the loss of his smile. I wonder should I be here, is it inviting him to backslide? and I suspect my motives in digging into his doctrine, is it to vie with the guru he needs more than me? but it's my nature to finger the print of the nails, is it a favor to him to swallow my doubt?—doubt too is a piece of the relative world which, not unlike a father, is the only one he has.

So another night I ask him, "Since these metabolic tests are quoted so much, why don't the researchers hook up Maharishi and publish the findings?"

He says promptly, "That would be sacrilege."

It's okay, the bond is intact, not snippable by me; and I'm both displeased and pleased.

32

So it was there, the idea of human relatedness, embedded in the commitment of disciple to master. Not a husband or father, Maharishi made a gracious bow to such roles, but it was with authority that he spoke as disciple and master; it was much in the tapes. But the tradition of that relationship—with the master needless of it, the disciples "kissing his lotus feet"—hardly included the two-day blow which broke over the twenty-second lecture.

The task that lecture undertook was to prove the transcendental was "intellectually locatable". Its logic was that waking, sleeping, dreaming, may be experienced in any of the twenty-four hours, and the "junction-point" between any two thus occurs anywhere and anytime; it is the "source and goal" of each. Between the ending of one state and the beginning of another the junction-point is unmanifest, unlike anything in the other three, which "are like curtains hiding it". The transcendental is not located in their character, but underlies them all. Since it issues in states which are conscious, the transcendental too must be conscious. But whereas they are different and changing, it is absolute and unchanging; and it may be reached from the waking state by a refinement of perception down to the junction-point, where the qualities of the other three will be transcended.

I had seen this tape in the crash "overview" before silence and figured my head was too cluttery, I'd follow the argument better next time; now, after a morning spent in crossing it three ways, I still saw it as proof by fiat. I went to our small group in the afternoon thinking I'd keep my big mouth shut.

Colorado said, "It's full of holes."

To which our leader, looking over his notes, coolly replied, "There are at least four logical fallacies here—"

And the talk was on, with everyone in the group poking fingers at this hole and that, just like nail prints. We broke it off to do our rote business, the questions-and-answers, but the intellectual dissatisfactions kept bubbling out. Bubbling wasn't enough, the group said that I "had the words" and should recapitulate theirs in the full session that evening.

I never got a chance. The meeting no sooner began than it was obvious the discontent had been rife in all the afternoon groups, and in two minutes the students from mine were erupting with everything they'd deputized me to say; the joint was jumping for a half-hour with quotes from philosophy, logic, the sciences. With the tape more or less in ribbons, one polite boy said of the doctrine:

"Not that any of this is false, but we'd be safer making brash statements."

It didn't end there, it was decided we should help Maharishi rewrite the tape; those interested in this arranged to meet the next day, but then a clinical psychologist took the floor for a brief talk on the philosophy of science and suggested the entire course be restructured to meet its dictates; and when the meeting broke up it had spawned a group who called themselves "the revisionists".

I left with a now troubled youth I knew, who told me a philosopher on the MIU staff had advised Maharishi the logic was flawed.

"Maharishi said see it again, and each time he saw it he went back to Maharishi and said it didn't hold up logically, and the eighth time Maharishi said then you better change your logic."

I said but I thought Maharishi invited specialists to bring him their "language"?

"I sometimes wonder," the young man said gloomily. "What everybody in that room is asking is whether Maharishi knows as much as he says he does."

"What does he say he knows?"

"That a man in unity can do anything."

I said, "I never heard him say that."

"Well, I did."

I went up to bed, and added the dialogue to the notes I had begun to keep. In the morning, I was accosted on the breakfast line by a young man whose face had a lot of hard living in it.

"You're a playwright, what do you do with this?"

"What do you mean?"

"If you can't knock the script *or* the star?"

It was a revolt of the angels, unthinkable in Maharishi's presence. When the three hundred of us were gathered in the hall, a teacher of philosophy in his thirties said he'd like to read a page inspired by the logic of yesterday's lecture—a mock bulletin on the silent dining-room which had never materialized. Standing between the two dark TV sets, he read it out to us:

It is common knowledge that we do not experience the Silent Dining Room. Therefore we can say that it is unmanifest. Because it is unmanifest we can intellectually conclude that it exists as the basis of all the activity at the grossest level of dining. Because the Silent Dining Room could be created at any moment, night or day, we know that it is eternal. Who knows where it might turn up? It could be created anywhere, in the Hotel Pato Rojo or in Block 7; thus we know it must be unbounded and absolute. The only question that remains is how to contact this pure, unmanifest, eternal, absolute Silent Dining Room.

The answer is the simple natural technique called Transcendental Mastication. Transcendental Mastication can be described as taking a bite that is suitable to the individual and experiencing it from the grossest eating level through subtler and subtler levels of munching until we transcend even the finest level of salivation.

Obviously therefore the Silent Dining Room ex-
ists in its pure unmanifest state as the junction-point
between any two bites!

This salvo was interrupted by howls of laughter
to the end; I followed him to his seat to copy it in
my notebook, and we settled down to the next two
tapes. The first dealt with subjective and objective
means of knowledge. The second was on speech,
and when Maharishi said the "power of speech is
that it binds the boundless"—a quote from the
Vedas—I thought yes, exactly, it capped a logic of
my own that I'd glimpsed two days earlier.

Throughout, the silence was as devoted as ever,
nothing had changed a whit. The revisionists met
at lunch, but without me, their work was to extend
into the weeks after I was gone; I never learned
whether any of it got to Maharishi's eye. In any
case, I had become a believer, though in a different
junction-point.

33

The point I'd made in my group about imagery—
"bare ruin'd choirs"—was in answer to the question,
how is creative intelligence "integrative"? The
correct words were that it integrated the absolute
and the relative, and I opened with them, but my
own experience was in the relative; I said we saw it
at work there too, in every image of a poem. In
"choirs" the poet brought together the diverse
worlds of botany and religion, the boughs that
shake against the cold and the pews empty of belief,
in one symbol of his aging. I myself thought the
point gratuitous; it took me a week to see it held
the answer to the big question nagging me.

As for pews, I was to kneel in so many with the
seminarian—after the course we made a three-day
tour of Andalusia—that I feared it was soon going
to seem reasonable by sheer force of habit. I told
myself mass was the only show in town, but I was
serious by then about something I'd glimpsed at the
heart of it in Punta Umbria.

The church there was a new yellowbrick edifice
on the river side of town; on our first Sunday four
of us went off to it before dinner. Angled to fit a
lot between stores selling outboard motors, it was

yellowbrick inside too, and bare as a garage; the one decorative touch in it was a garish nine-foot statue of Christ, hanging on the brick wall at front, so burly of biceps and thighs that I thought he looked more like the savior of the San Diego Chargers. In this merciless room I expected no movement of the heart, and I sat bored through mass, as adrift in Spanish as I had been in the Latin of my childhood.

But in that moment when the padre elevated in his fingers the host, a wafer large as a saucer, and greedily ate it, I experienced a tremor of revulsion and my eyes blurred with tears. It was cannibalistic, under that brawny sacrifice on the cross, but for the first time in my life I comprehended the unity of the wafer and the body of Christ and the spirit; not only magic, it was prayer, a beseeching that the perfection of the unique life which haunted our history might become our flesh. I had never before "seen" the doctrine of transubstantiation or the nature of prayer. For prayer itself was not what I'd thought—more magic, as when my wife at six had stood with palm out and eyes closed, thinking if there's a God let him put a Baby Ruth in my hand —but another means to alter our state of consciousness.

My companions and the Spaniards of the town, having exchanged the "kiss of peace", moved up to the altar steps to eat the divine flesh themselves. I sat in the pew and watched; but a hunger for that wafer was to trouble me thereafter. It seemed like the egg and not the shell. It was so sharp a moment that it stayed with me the next few days, a "message" I was not to hear again in any church; in midweek I awoke long before dawn and knew I understood, not everything, but something.

34

Well, it was all of a piece, including that devout housewife, my mother. I mean, what other body is broken and blood shed that each of us might live? —the wafer was avowedly an invocation to rebirth, and at least one of my tears was for my original host.

So, born in the ruins of that unity, we take our first breath and look for one plum or another; God is a hunger, and unity is the food. Unity is the transcendence of conflict. Seek, and ye shall find. My moment with the wafer, and my friend's homily at Christmas, "inasmuch as ye have done it unto one of the least of these", and my nineteenth year in the exaltation of the brotherhood of communism, yea, sisterhood too, and my others atop the Colorado mountains or over a crib or in Israel, and the recovered unity with my son here—each was a turn of the heart urgent enough to overflow and transmute conflict, a minute I dare think in and out of God; I hadn't been left out. Ye shall find because, says one saint, "he who seeks God has already found him."

But most of my life was a writer's, hunched over a pencil and paper, what is that? At its most opportunistic it's piecework, a dollar a scribble, supplying a market; its reward then is in the dollar, the fruits of action. But if it's what a writer calls "my own work"—say, making a poem for which no market exists—it is identical with prayer, a means to alter his own state of consciousness. With this observation, offered by my son about work of mine, we come back to the voices in a playwright's head.

And here, while borrowing from my family, I interpolate a leaf from my wife's book, in progress, a psychoanalytic examination of the creative process in one playwright and his plays. In it she makes a discovery which is a revelation to me—whatever else a play is about, it is unwittingly also about the writer's creative process. In the model of the form we looked at a while back—"the son as playwright uses it to discover truth"—it is at the heart of the action. Rarely so overt, it lurks in furtive places, but few plays will not yield it. This leaf goes into the pot for a good bit more than flavor.

In the playwright's head, or any man's, the voices of the past are infinite—the undigested odds and ends of his lifetime, a bedlam of the sights, sounds, touches of the world since his first breath and the multitudinous bubbles of desires, thoughts, feelings in him; he is a ferment of incompatibilities. But it's slumbrous, and the playwright walks around like everyman in an uneasy equilibrium, twenty percent awake. The equilibrium is a survival built upon a suppressing until—as in the play itself: I said it was an image of the mind—it is broken into by a "happening", the perception of that ghost we call form, which bodes some strange eruption to our state; it unbinds the energies locked in the equilibrium, and the eruption is the play.

I've spoken of working badly as life's chief burden, and of working well as its chief delight; there is a third state, working too well. In a more rapturous era the word was inspiration. It's a kind of seizure, by that simultaneity of insight and design we looked at earlier, and artists live for it; it's when they know they're most alive. Every writer has flashes of it, even in his hack work, though dimly there. In writing poems I've had the fit for a few hours, when lucky enough to complete one at a sitting, and for a few days too; more often it comes and goes, leaving me with patches of hard work in between. But I've been through several stretches in my life—each with a play—when for a month or two the fit took over and ran me so mercilessly I thought its designs were perhaps on my sanity.

It begins joyously, with an excitement of the blood, after the deadlock of silence; the words, characters, scenes flow like living water from the rock. They rise from the depths, unplanned, and full of surprises. Not usually identifiable, one fragment may be from a childhood day at grandma's, another is yesterday's joke in lovemaking, a third is from a funeral twenty years ago; they fit together like jigsaw pieces in one scene. Their origins are of no interest, what matters is their unity. Nor is it only scattered times and places that fit; the segregated strata of the heart so melt and interflow that in one breath the most tearful grief and the funniest joke come up together, two sides of a nugget. All this is emotional, the opening of consciousness downward, a dissolution of old "boundaries"; but simultaneously there is an intellectual widening upward, a vision of new boundaries without precedent—form—within which these diversities are happily wedded, one flesh. The intellect's reach is extended, and its control is swift, more cunning, "spontaneously right"; it is unerring in how it proportions and places the materials, and each problem of structure shows up hand in hand with its solution. And all the misfortunes of the past are so usable, and so unsubstitutable, they seem like the sheerest of good luck. Or, teleological?—like religion. Suffering ends; the old griefs, genuine enough, are felt now as pieces of creative joy. It is even embarrassing.

This eruption of voices and images outruns the playwright's ability to get them on paper. He has no time to waste on the other pleasures of life, which indeed seem minor, because he falls behind the dialogue he "overhears"; I'm constantly jotting down scraps of it from future scenes I won't get to for days or weeks. Here the future co-exists with the intent of the past, time itself is a unity. An hour away from the desk is hazardous, I may miss a voice, and the murmurings of the flesh for food and rest are impertinences. A mouthful is a meal, the stomach won't digest more. I go to bed tired out, but after four hours am awakened by the clamor of characters chasing each other around in my skull, and get back to my desk; I am at it before dawn and till after midnight. The body seems to crave stimulants—coffee and tobacco—to keep up with the mind, until the belly is sour and the tongue sore. Such lack of sleep, semi-fasting, dosing with mild drugs, conspire to feed the exhilaration; but mainly it feeds itself, discovery breeding discovery, consciousness widening inward and outward.

It is beatific for a week or two, then turns oppressive. The body and mind tire, the inspiration does not. In such a fit of twenty-hour workdays I have finished the latter half of a full-length play, been unable to stop, and gone on to write all of another; in six weeks I dropped fifteen pounds and felt outrageously used—in fact, hag-ridden; what began as a blessing ends as a nightmare, like the ballet slippers that won't come off but keep dancing. Now a touch of terror is in it, so tenuous are my ties to the earth and so manic my buoyance that any hour I may float away into heaven like a toy balloon, and never get back. I don't, instead I collapse into a bout of flu that anchors me in bed for a week.

It becomes, in brief, a "bad trip"—because how I describe inspiration is how the students I ask describe good trips, and with equal ease their words translate into the lexicon of the movement. "This is it," or the absolute; "basic, life itself," or pure consciousness; you are "liberated", from former

suffering; "all the conflicts are resolved," or mon-
ism. You travel into "light, energy, power," which
translates, to the source of all energy. You are
flooded with "joy", translated as bliss, and "love"
which is purely creative, bleached of its darker
side. You "don't need sleep", and the "boundaries"
between things—a glass and a table, or your skin
and the sea—dissolve, and you "know who you are",
synonymous with the universal intelligence; so you
feel a "oneness" with everything, which translates,
the subject and the object unite. And then you
"come down", not with the flu, but with a "crash".

Otherwise, this adds up to a rough definition of
"unity consciousness". For a few days I hesitated
to equate that happy state with the creative fit—
which point for point coincides with every quality
of Maharishi's "creative intelligence", it too is integrative, progressive, purposeful, discriminative,
"infallible", selectively precise, innovative, orderly,
and self-sufficient, creating everything from within
itself. But after three days came the videotape in
which he quoted the Vedas, "The power of speech
is that it binds the boundless," as in all its properties
of form I have described. I thought yes, exactly, am
I so wrong?—and two tapes later, halfway into his
talk on science and art, I knew I wasn't; Maharishi
said, "The artist strikes from the transcendental
level of his own life."

Eureka! we meant the same thing, the oneness in
a playwright's head. Or did we? All of a piece it
was, neither had I been left out here, and I'd written

162

my wife, "I think I've got it, what Maharishi's talking about, and it may very well be true"—he was delineating a state of mind which I now knew existed. Yet a worm of doubt nibbled at my pleasure. What, what?

Something was backwards. The playwright lives, suffers, works in the relative. The outward structure of a play—his design of struggle, will against will, mounting to a resolution which includes both in a new equilibrium—is the image of his inner struggle to "make sense" of his life, and not by a suppressing; the contradictory voices of his play are echoes of the debate which opened in him at birth. I say play, but mean poem too, or any artwork. The working-out of forces in conflict, common to all, is most naked in a play; it is a "special case", in which the diversities to be integrated are in head-on collision. It's no accident that the end is what the playwright often sees first. That is, the resolution is visible before the conflict is; and when the end is not soon visible the work aborts—the inspiration dies. Why? I think its energies put the writer in jeopardy, they are his insanity, and come to the surface only when he can bind them; what invites them is his perception of the form; but thereafter they are in the saddle, a demon rider, and flog him on to the end, their leap out of conflict into unity.

And if he is wrong?—his life is a bet on that horse, the leap against the voices in the pit, and it's common enough to find him stumbling in the ranks of the casualties, drunks, aberrants, suicides; the arts are a tribe of the walking wounded.

If he is not wrong, the form is a safe-conduct through his hell. But form, we have seen, is that social shaping which "communicates", and permits —more, obliges—the audience to feel what the playwright has felt. It draws us in, like a net, and scene by scene we make the journey with him into a landscape at war, tragic or comic, but mirroring an underworld in ourselves to which we are otherwise blind; and it leads us out into a daylight of widened "oneness". Vicarious conflict, his play is a safe-conduct through our hell too, a pale reflection of his. For which we love the artist, and support him, and hate his guts.

That art and religion are housemates, we've always known; he has led us into that "archetype of wholeness" in the unconscious whose "central position"—says the psychoanalyst of archetypes—"approximates it to the God-image". Or, to quote his forerunner by five hundred years, "beyond the coincidence of contradictories" where alone God "may be seen, and nowhere this side thereof".

But in art we are talking of a genesis in diversity, and unity is its manifestation; in this philosophy— or any religion—we begin with the unity, and diversity is its manifestation. The something backwards was this reversal, and to see its consequences I sketched them out in a diagram, which surprised me. I apologize for it, to the printer and reader, but my surprise was visual. Besides, it looks scientific.

First half, metaphysics. The absolute is unmani-

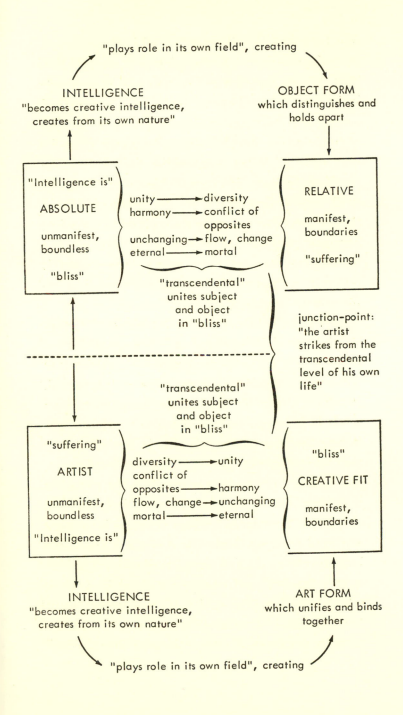

fest, boundless, Intelligence "is". It is characterized by unity—harmony, unchanging and eternal. It is bliss. When Intelligence "prepares to play a role in its own field, existence becomes conscious and Intelligence becomes intelligent"; that is, it "becomes creative intelligence, and creates from its own nature". What it creates is the play of the manifest. Subject, it creates objects—in "boundaries", whose function is to distinguish and hold them apart. Now the unity shows itself in diversity; harmony gives birth to the conflict of opposites; the unchanging becomes flow, change; the eternal is manifest in the mortal. But the transcendental informs both worlds, it unites subject and object.

Second half, fact. Prior to his work, the playwright's mind is "unmanifest", boundless; his intelligence "is". It is characterized by diversity—the conflict of opposites, flow and change; it is mortal. It suffers. When his intelligence "prepares to play a role in its own field" by the act of writing, "existence becomes conscious", that is, buried matters rise; his intelligence "becomes creative intelligence, and creates from its own nature". What it creates is the manifest of the play. Subject, it creates the object—in "boundaries", whose function is to unify and bind together. Now the diversities are mated in unity; the conflict of opposites gives birth to harmony; the flow and change are fixed in a work which is unchanging. And if it's not eternal, he at least thinks it is—"not marble, nor the gilded monuments of princes, shall outlive this powerful rhyme."

166

But in the creative fit he and the work are one; "like to like", subject and object unite, "free from doubts about life".

Now, putting these halves together and reading from the midline up and down, what do we see?

Everything is backwards! Tabulated so, the metaphysics and the creative process mirror each other, in reverse; and the reversal reaches into their sequels. In both, we return to the "unmanifest"—in one the absolute, in the other the artist's daily life. But in the philosophy the enlightenment is "being", and it grows; its end is serenity. In creativity the fit is "doing", and it burns itself out; its end is exhaustion. Permanent, temporary. Fulfilled, the enlightened dwell in bliss; fulfilled, the artist goes back to—at best, a higher level of—his struggle.

And the man-god nailed to his cross?—he is the agonist of another metaphysics, and hangs at the crux of both worlds, absolute and relative. Here there are two stories, of course. In the first, Jehovah is the boundless, and creates from his own nature the play of history which is his manifestation; subject and object separate, and suffering—conflict, change, mortality—appears with man's disobedience and exile, but obedience to the tablets will restore the promised land. That kingdom fails, however. It is succeeded by the messianic hope, of unity again with Jehovah, and so the second story. Now the manifestation is a unique phenomenon in the people's history, a relative object which is also boundless—the only-begotten son who is man "in all things except sin" and thus, although he suffers, has conflict, is mortal, always is capable of obedience to the death; inseparable from deity, inseparable from humanity, he reunites subject and object by embracing all sin and suffering on the cross. Complicated by its marriage to history and a young deity who is much more a storyteller and poet than an It, this cosmology is also squeezable into the diagram—comprises, if we take him as artist, both halves.

Well, a diagram is not reality, whatever else is, and we can throw it away after a last look. In this mirror we can read the reflection of truth and fiction either way. Is the metaphysical the true state of affairs?—then the artist, haunted by its intimations in this world, creates in his work an image of the eternal. So, later in the Alhambra I heard that the first Sultan to occupy it said in wonder, "If this is earth, what must heaven be?" Is this life the true state of affairs?—then man creates in his vision of the eternal an image of his own creativity. And we are back to a threadbare debate, did God make man in his likeness, or vice versa? Believers and doubters, perhaps this man is surer when authority is external and that man when it is internal.

But in my wife's book the writer, whatever his overt theme of conflict, includes the covert theme of creativity. Is this only the narcissism of the artist?—it may be rather that the creative is the essence of the human. I take it that, in considering the relative and the absolute, man and God, we are no longer talking about some geography external to the human mind. If the creative is truly our essence, what deeper eye in us would we call on when speculating about the mystery we are born into?—and it would not be improbable to find the artist's creativity is the archetype and pattern for all cosmology.

In any case, if we are to believe my wife, the scriptures of the world were written by men who were writers.

35

One day now in the first row there is a new girl, brunette, pale and remote; she sits through both tapes with downcast eyes.

Next morning in the same chair she kneels facing the back of the hall, with a knowing smile on her lips—I'm uneasy at what it contains, or won't, a hint of some demon rider after a spurious unity. Next session, kneeling backwards throughout the lecture, she smiles more openly and pantomimes conversation and waves a hand to someone invisible; our young leader beside her murmurs a word, she settles down. Not sure he understands, I go to him after the lecture with a keen observation:

"Something's wrong with her."

"Yes. The doctors know."

I see no doctors, but they are more vigilant than I think.

Around midnight my son and I, talking in my room, are startled by a screaming somewhere, and we go quickly into the hall; a handful of others are hurrying out of their rooms, uncertain. The screaming is downstairs.

Colorado says, "Someone's freaking out!"

I know who, that knowing smile is in pieces,

and several of us start down; at the turn of the stairs we are met by a young woman I've never seen, who blocks us with a hand and an accent.

"Please. It is all right."

I ask, "Are you the doctor?"

"No, the nurse. The doctor is with her. Please, go back."

So we do, and thereafter all is quiet.

In a day or two I see the girl again, sitting alone in the lobby, mute but more normal; the pieces are coming together—it's as if the demon made a leap, fell back, and is settling for a more modest unity—and the next morning she is on the food line in sporadic talk with someone in the flesh. In the lobby that evening I spy the doctor I know, whom I like, and ask him how unstressing of such magnitude is dealt with, sedation? I take his answer to show a sensible minimality:

"Not if we can avoid it. We did massage and kept her talking all night."

Later in the week at the food table I run into the girl, tray to tray; now her face is candid, and I note her tray is full.

I say politely, "How are you?"

"Fine," she says in some surprise. "How are you?"

36

I was fine too, I at last knew where I stood, a defender of the faith or at least its backside. In a minor classic of our day there's a fox who thinks men are curiously limited, their only interests are hunting foxes and raising chickens; if I was running with the fox, it was nonetheless a treat.

I should have been embarrassed, haunting the premises like the ghost of that deposed king to "set it right" myself, usurping my wife on the creativity side and my son on the cosmic; we needn't mention the new king. Instead, I felt saintly. The doctrine says one becomes "more tolerant and accepting" with higher consciousness—logical, if higher means the inclusion of further opposites. I'd been loving enough, what with the sea and the pleasurable faces around me and my firstborn, a true prophet, his "love and warmth" were real. But once I saw the doctrine as joinable to my life I went into a higher gear, exhilarated at dropping my various skunks into the pot together—the healing, the assorted messianic hopes, the exaltation itself, many diversities now a unity—and, thinking I might serve them up in a little book, I too was "living the knowledge". Only

Castro and the Spanish glory remained to be accounted for.

In our last week some weariness was setting in among the others. The questions furnished to the small groups were answerable by the same phrases day after day, and in mine no one now was writing small essays; five or six words were thrown out in a kind of shorthand, which sufficed. In the large group, the weariness took a humorous turn.

Each lecture was introduced by a harpsichord on the sound track, a stately tinkling, until one morning the youth at the dials blasted off with a Viennese waltz. As training, different students now stood in for our leader in dictating the summaries we wrote down; irreverent cries of "Slower!" grew customary, and bred cries of "Faster!" and soon every new reader was plagued by a chorus of "Slower! Faster! Slower!"—undergraduate horseplay. In one videotape Maharishi was at last outwitted by a flower, lifting it from others he drew up an unsightly dangle of stems he couldn't shake loose of, and for several sentences—on some virtue of enlightenment—his unavailing efforts to get free of it convulsed the students. Not without some guilt. When he was into a long quote in Sanskrit a voice called out, "Slower!" and there was laughter, but several others said, "Sssh!" and it died at once. Three boys in orbit around a witty girl had founded a "negativity club", pledged they said to a loftier affirmativity. Its official papers included cartoons in their notebooks—as, two large TV sets droning "ZZZZZ" at a roomful of little TV sets droning "zzzzz"—and a dummy sentence of great complexity whose every other clause was a multiple-choice blank, to be filled in with slugs of favorite phraseology; in any combination it made "just as good sense", and was to be resorted to when listeners who didn't understand you the first time asked you to clarify, you offered it again in a new combination.

But for me the phraseology had become fresh, with personal meanings. Thus when Maharishi said, "For the artist every step of progress in the creation of his art is a step towards greater realization of the values of the Creator," I thought he'd been spying on me at mass. I was left with the enigma of his own state of enlightenment, which I was not to solve; I toyed with the notion that all of us were characters in a world drama being written by him, laid at the dead feet of his beloved Guru Dev, with Maharishi in a chronic high of inspiration. I was perhaps not too far off: later I was to hear his own view of that death, Maharishi had been for thirteen years "a small planet" circling the sun and one day "the sun vanished—what does a planet do?" But the real gap was between my experience of a fitful unity in the resolution of conflicts, and his of a steady unity prior to conflicts. And if so, I thought, can you get there from here?—of course, said the orthodox, follow the leader. But the question turned on the word "experience"; his was not known to me. Or to any of the others. No one I asked had ever heard Maharishi say what degree of consciousness he was in, he played his cards mighty close to his dhoti, and I guessed maybe it was as with western men of the cloth; for one to claim he was in a state of grace would at once disprove it, those I knew were hoping. Hope was the writing on the pillars—could it be there was nothing knowable more than that extraordinary sentence, "He who seeks God has already found him"? It could be. In any case, I was bright and bushy-tailed with my new understanding, however partial, and came to my small group full of clever thoughts; one was that I was talking too much in it.

But the metaphysics was a vast new meadow in which to romp, and great fun. In his twenty-ninth lecture on "horizontal and vertical" knowledge, Maharishi included Newton and his apple in the vertical—not its fall, the depth of the insight—and following that thread of thought I found Castro at the end of it, and finally got him too into the pot.

The mantra was only one means of transcending; Maharishi said the human nervous system was "the dynamic element" in the universe, and any "boundary" in the relative, pursued to its end, would lead us into the absolute. In the large group I was invited to explicate this, and I spoke at some learned length about Newton, of whose work I know absolutely nothing. But mathematics is the "language" of one such boundary, and Newton was a master of it. For aeons, millions of men had seen apples fall to the earth, and for millions of mornings had seen the

sun cross the sky—diverse and unconnected phenomena; Newton, via mathematics, saw a formula
which related not only the apple to the earth but
the earth to the sun, and thereafter the apple's fall
and the sun's rise were, for all men, two manifestations of a single reality; matter had become mind.
To effect a new unity of apple and sun did not in
nature differ from the artist's reconciliation of his
diversities. In our cosmology, Newton had "transcended" and brought back into the relative a piece
of the absolute, hitherto not a part of man's knowledge.

The terminology thus suggested another definition of "genius", a man whose mastery of one language is so profound that by means of it he delivers
into the manifest a piece of the unmanifest—one
could say the same of Beethoven's. And wasn't this
exactly what the students saw as Maharishi's gift
to them? In history's parade of charismatic leaders,
most of them revolutionaries, not one but must
convince his following he has transcended the bond-
age of their limits; he brings out of his unmanifest
some unity, political or spiritual, not before available to them; his vision reconciles the diversities
their lesser talents cannot. Castro or Maharishi, then,
the leader is serving his followers precisely as the
artist serves his audience.

I said to one such follower I sometimes felt Maharishi was holding back on half his thoughts.

"Half?" said the student. "He's not telling us one
percent of what he knows!"

In the last two days, rounding was permitted again, and the students let out a cheer; my son's face perked up. Now, in the evening, the interlude for discussion between tapes was taken over by floor-talk of the day's experiences in rounding, some of them oddities—perseverant imagery, illusions of floating and bodily expansion or shrinkage, eye pains and blackouts and tongue swellings—but all explained as "unstressing", the dissolution of psychic knots. Usually, such sessions would be presided over by Maharishi himself, and I saw there was a department of psychotherapy I was to remain ignorant of. I wasn't in on this new cycle, I was to take the final exam and leave.

But why do I speak only of the therapy as theirs? —the fact is, I was leaving in better shape myself. Brimful of hints and guessings, I was on the intriguing edge of a new frontier in my experience; I had half considered it was over. Live and learn, I wasn't very different from the widow who had " a new man in her life".

The one in my eye was that harrowing figure of the word become flesh on a cross in the monastery: he knew something profound about the oneness within that we were hankering after. It wasn't happenstance that so much of Maharishi's talk was a peacemaking; the students questioned him about the cosmic, or what in my day we called "pie in the sky", but he always answered between the two worlds, keeping both; the unity of opposites—artist and scientist, east and west, subject and object, absolute and relative—was his great text. It wasn't happenstance that enlightenment in the east meant transcending the narcissism of the individual ego, and that the epochal instance of it in the west hung in every church. It wasn't happenstance, the new ecumenicalism in them—when I got back to a mass in my own tongue I asked a priest, "How did all this Protestantism get into our church?"—and their radical theologians of God's death were also reaching across a gulf to the "atheistic" religions of the east. Something was in the wind of a sick world, a pentecostal stir, the slumbrous mind of man groping. For a form, for a form. It was quite a play, I hoped its authors were equal to the coming act; meanwhile I had a consuming interest in the wafer.

On my last afternoon I took a towel and walked a mile up the low-tide beach, stripped, and dunked myself a few times in the sea, a leavetaking. In my small group we had a "party", we all chipped in a few pesetas and shared an ice-cream cake. And in my room that night I wined and crackered the meditators of the monastery trip, including of course my son; in these weeks I'd noticed a change in us too for the better, a paradox, I felt closer to him at a distance. I had no worries now, what he'd found of himself in this movement would be his for keeps. But I was flying half a world away from some of my flesh, so of course I said geography didn't matter.

"Isn't love being in the same state of consciousness?"

"I guess," he said with his smile.

Nevertheless.

In the morning I wrote the exam paper in my room, a two-hour essay on the cardinal points of the ideology, and packed my suitcase. My son stepped in for a goodbye handshake, and studied the room, with my ghost already in its corners.

"How noisy is it here?"

He was debating the eternal question, to move or not to move, and he solved it minimally, on the john. On which sentimental scene we parted; I had hired a cab to Seville, and I took my suitcase down to it.

37

And so goodbye to Punta Umbria, which I am not likely to see again and don't care, even with its new sewer lines in.

I had three passengers in the cab, and one we dropped off in Seville to catch a plane; the other two were my young friends, the seminarian and the Canadian girl, whom I'd invited along for a look at Andalusia. For three days we wandered in the mosques and cathedrals of Cordoba, Granada, Cadiz, and went to mass once a day together, sometimes twice, and slept for ninety cents a night, not together, and ate a variety of delicious fish-soups everywhere, and back in Seville hugged each other goodbye. They drove south to Punta Umbria; I flew north to Madrid, visited the Prado, went alone to mass, and boarded my jet for home.

We winged over the snow-sprinkled sierras of Spain. Which had sent those three bottlecork ships ahead of me so long ago, and out of its civil wars— I understood its glory now—came of age in all its unity and greatness; a century later its invincible fleet sank in the Channel, and England after its civil wars came of age in all its unity and greatness, spawning its America; which a century and a half later broke free, and after its civil war came of age in all its unity and greatness, from which our students had fled. Individuals, nations, it was all of a piece—the hour in which inner conflict is transcended is that of the exaltation. As in the theatre.

The stewardess came down the aisle with copies of the *New York Times*, my first look at the news in six weeks. In Washington, a senator had been shot and robbed in his driveway; in northern Ireland, five more were dead of Christian differences; in Indochina, the planes the senator had sponsored were seeding the villages with bombs, bombs, bombs; in New York, the police had succeeded in stealing from themselves $73,000,000 worth of heroin, vanished into the arms of the city—and so on, page after page, the people of the day running around like decapitated chickens; and when I turned to the arts, half the ads were of pornographic movies. I was back in the real world.

Sure was great to get away from them crazy kids.

Well, where had I been?—on a ferry ride to nowhere, into the mind, to everywhere. I kept forgetting it; with a headful of God, art, gravitation, history, eternity, nationality, I caught myself thinking of the absolute and the relative as entities in some space or time. Mind, mind, they were mind, form, the shell in which we contain the egg. In an early tape Maharishi said something about creative intelligence which now was not gibberish; cross-legged, with his cupped hand before his heart, unmoving, he said, "Its range is from here to here, passing through there, which is also here." So that's where I'd been, where I'd always been, but never before.

And so flew on home, where there was nothing new under the sun, or old either.

WILLIAM GIBSON

A Season in Heaven is William Gibson's third "chronicle," following *The Seesaw Log* and *A Mass for the Dead*. He has also published a novel, *The Cobweb*, poetry, and a half-dozen plays, including *Two for the Seesaw* and *The Miracle Worker*, and is the co-author of two sons. He has lived for twenty-six years in the Berkshires of Massachusetts, where his new play, *The Body & the Wheel*, was produced this spring.